Stitched HOLIDAY ORNAMENTS

25+ *beaded treasures*

Thomasin Alyxander

Kalmbach Media

Kalmbach Media
21027 Crossroads Circle
Waukesha, Wisconsin 53186
www.JewelryAndBeadingStore.com

Numbered illustrations by the author. Lettered step-by-step photographs by Nedda Rovelli. All other photography © 2020 Kalmbach Media except where otherwise noted.

Published in 2020
24 23 22 21 20   1 2 3 4 5

Manufactured in China

ISBN: 978-1-62700-761-0
EISBN: 978-1-62700-762-7

Editor: Erica Barse
Book Design: Lisa Schroeder
Assistant Editor: Katie Salatto
Technical Editor: Julia Gerlach
Photographer: William Zuback
Proofreader: Dana Meredith

Library of Congress Control Number: 2019950856

Table of CONTENTS

Introduction

My favorite part of Christmas has always been the tree. Unpacking the ornaments and arranging them on the tree is like seeing old friends and relatives again. In my family, everyone has a couple of designated ornaments that we are supposed to hang, and there are some ornaments that we try to be lucky enough to find and hang before anyone else does. Most ornaments have a story that goes with them—who gave it to whom, the trip during which an ornament was purchased, who made it, and other places our memories take us. Decorating the tree is a grand way for us to reconnect and ready ourselves for the holiday season.

I wrote this book so you could start ornament stories for yourself and the people in your life. Each project has meaning for me—and you and your family and friends will give your own meanings to them. While you work on an ornament, think of it as a place where nostalgia and an heirloom will meet. For years to come, people will hang that ornament and be reminded of you, an event, or even a place. As Christmas trees come and go, these ornaments will remind people of past holidays, as well as everyone and everything that makes a holiday a holiday. Perhaps one day, some day in the future, someone you never met will pause to think about you and the time you dedicated to the ornament.

Perhaps you hate to see something you've worked on with such devotion put away for months at a time? These ornaments don't have to be relegated to the decoration box. Let the story be told however and wherever you want it to be told. The story is yours.

—Alyx

BASICS

thread

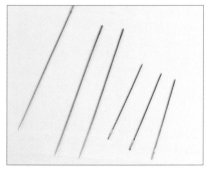

needles

seed beads

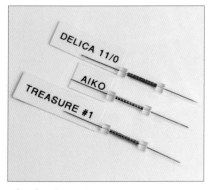

other beads

THREAD AND NEEDLES

Thread

Although you can use whatever bead-weaving thread you prefer—and there are a lot of options—I only tested three kinds: Toho One-G, Miyuki K. O. and C-Lon AA. These threads are slightly thinner than size D thread, but they seem to be equally strong. If the instructions say you can use any size D thread or an equivalent, you do not have to use these threads. If they do say to use one of these threads, that is because I am not certain that a regular size D thread can make the number of passes necessary at some point in the ornament. Also, regular size D thread sometimes does not allow an ornament cover to have the proper drape. If this is your first foray into bead weaving, I recommend using one of the three tested threads. Just be sure you stretch these threads before doing any bead weaving. Pull the recommended length of thread between your hands, working your way from one end to the other. You'll know you've stretched it properly if the thread is no longer curly. Make sure you use a comparable size of thread if you substitute a thread for one of the three listed above.

Needles

Use a needle to pick up small beads such as seed beads and cylinder beads. Feel free to use whatever size needle is comfortable for you after checking to see if a particular size is recommended. I like to keep on hand sizes 10, 11, 12, and 15 so I can switch to a thinner needle if I get in a tight spot. Be sure to use the long beading needles and good quality needles such as John James or Tulip. For most projects, a long needle will be better. You may prefer to use short beadking needles for the bead embroidery projects.

Conditioner

I'm still using up a box of Thread Heaven I've been using for ages. Unfortunately, Thread Heaven closed their doors a few years ago, so their silicone conditioner is no longer available. Thread Magic is supposed to be very similar, and I've also heard that you can use silicone ear plugs — but rumor has it that the silicone in ear plugs MIGHT damage thread over time. Beeswax is what I used before discovering Thread Heaven, and it works well. After you have stretched the thread, condition it by pulling it through beeswax or a silicone conditioner. If you use beeswax, run the thread between your nails to strip off any unsightly blobs of wax.

BEADS

Seed Beads and Cylinder Beads

Use only good quality Japanese seed beads, such as Toho or Miyuki. Keep on the lookout for beads that are obviously bigger, smaller, or irregularly shaped— discard these beads so you don't accidentally use them.

These projects use the standard size 11º Delica cylinder beads, and I've given color names to guide you. Toho Treasures 11º will give you excellent results as well. If you have access to Aikos and can afford them, by all means use them! They are lovely to work with. As you can see in the photo, these three different cylinder beads are very similar in size and shape.

Other Beads

You'll find many traditional accent beads in these designs, including crystals and pearls. Some ornaments are made with two-hole beads as well. These beads have trade names, and you cannot substitute a different bead for the one given. For example, I used SuperDuos as well as CzechMates tile and triangle beads in some projects.

NOTE I encourage you to visit your local bead stores to see if they have what you need. If they don't, I recommend Caravan Beads (caravanbeads.com) for Miyuki seed beads (including Delicas), as well as Ultrasuede for bead embroidery. Caravan also carries the C-Lon AA thread. I like Nicole's Bead Backing for embroidery (beadwright.com). Bobby Beads (bobbybead.net) is an excellent source for Toho seed beads and cylinder beads; they also have a good selection of two-hole beads. Out on a Whim (whimbeads.com) also carries a large selection of two-hole beads, seed beads, and Delicas. Potomac Beads (potomacbeads.com) is another good source for two-hole beads, beading foundations, thread, as well as Miyuki and Toho seed beads.

roundnose pliers

MISCELLANEOUS TOOLS

You'll need thread snips — make sure they are sharp. A thread burner can be handy if you can't quite trim a thread short enough, but they are very much an optional tool. A pair of chainnose pliers can be handy if you're having trouble pulling a needle through a bead. Make sure the needle is not genuinely stuck because you can break a bead if you force a needle through a hole that is too small or too full.

A couple of the projects do require a little wireworking to finish them. For these, you will need a pair of roundnose pliers, a pair of chainnose pliers, and a pair of flush cutters. You may also want to have a pair of 1mm chainnose pliers, although these are not strictly necessary.

chainnose pliers

STOP BEADS

Choose an 11º seed bead that is very different in color from the ones used in your project. Sew through it again so that you can see a thread on the outside of the bead. Avoid sewing through the thread while sewing through the bead again. Slide the bead down to where the instructions say. If the bead won't slide, you have sewn through the thread. Remove the bead and try again.

flush cutters

WORKSPACE

Plenty of good lighting is essential. Most people find that it's helpful to have directed light from a lamp as well as being in a reasonably well-lit space. You also need a mat of some kind to use as a beading surface. My personal favorite is a velux mat — it's a thinner version of those blankets that are often used in motels. There are other mats that have raised sides, and these are great for preventing your beads from rolling off the mat and onto the floor. Other people like to use a tray of some kind that is lined with either a display board or mat that has been cut to fit. Avoid anything with a hard edge because you can hurt your wrists if you make it a habit of resting them on the hard edge. Many beaders find it useful to label their mats with the names or codes of the beads in a project. This is a good way to keep from getting mixed up if you are using several beads of different colors that are the same size and to identify beads that may be new to you. Use clear tape and write the name of the bead (or its size or symbol) on the tape. Some people like to put the labels below or alongside the beads it is identifying; I like to put the tape above.

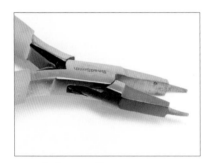

1mm chainnose pliers

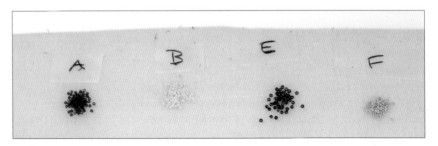

workspace

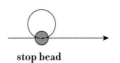

stop bead

how to make a hanger

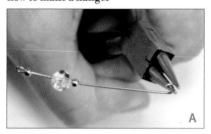

ORNAMENT BALLS AND HANGERS

Ornament Balls

Ornament covers never lose their appeal. I leave them up year-round and people always ask about them. A cover can drape or wrap around a plain glass ball; a cover can even perch on the ball. Dangles with weight help draw the cover down and encourage a draping cover to hang properly. Thread is also important. I only use Toho One-G or K. O. thread for covers. Regular size D threads can be too thick to allow the cover to drape effectively. Bonded threads sometimes have too much spring for a good drape to occur, especially if the dangles don't have enough weight. One way I help the dangles have weight is to use pewter bead caps. I prefer to use TierraCast bead caps in my covers because they are superbly finished and add appeal to the completed cover. I have learned the hard way to use gold- or rhodium-plated caps because silver ones will tarnish and it is very difficult to polish tiny bead caps.

Sometimes the cover will not go onto the glass ball if the seed beads used in the initial ring came from a production run that was on the thin side of the company's accepted sizing. If this happens, remove the metal cap from the glass ball. Put your cover on, pinch the cap where it sits on the shoulder of the ball, and coax it inside the top ring of the cover's beads.

Hangers

Have some ¼-in. (6mm) ribbon on hand — this will make the best hanger for many of the ornaments. You can also use a standard ornament hanger or make one out of a 20-gauge eye pin. You will need roundnose and chainnose pliers as well as a steel block, a chasing hammer, and some sort of a mandrel in order to make your own hangers. A fat pen often works quite well as a mandrel.

Start by sliding whatever beads you like onto the eye pin and down to the eye. Use roundnose pliers to put a "P" loop at the other end of the wire **(A)**. Use chainnose pliers to make a right-angle bend in the pin. Note that you hold the wire slightly away from the last bead, not right next to it. Make sure that the beads and the "P" loop are on the same side of the wire when you make this bend **(B)**. Shape the hanger into a hook around the dowel, making sure the "P" loop will end up on the outside of the hook **(C)**. Place only the hook part of the hanger flat on the block and hammer it lightly to stiffen the hook **(D)**.

TECHNIQUES

The projects in this book use a variety of stitches, materials, and techniques. If a technique is unfamiliar to you or you haven't done it in a while, take the time to review the technique in the basics section. If a project has a peculiar aspect to a stitch, that feature will be addressed in the specific project.

PEYOTE STITCH

Many of the ornaments in this book use peyote stitch because it is wonderfully versatile with many variations. In case this is the first time you're using peyote stitch, here are a two guidelines to keep in mind: You pick up the first TWO rows' worth of beads to begin stitching flat and tubular peyote stitches. In the third and each following row, the bead you pick up sits on top of a bead and you sew through the bead next to the one the new bead is sitting on. What often confuses people is that beads next to each other in peyote stitch are not in the same rows **(figure 1)**.

Tubular Peyote

This stitch always starts with an even number of beads and, as usual, you pick up the first two rows of beads to begin. You can either sew through all the beads again or tie a knot. Whichever you do, keep your tension soft and sew through the first bead you picked up again. The instructions may call for you sew through another bead as well. Pick up beads and sew through beads according to the chart or instructions. It can be easy to lose track of where you are so you may need to develop a personal trick to aid you, such as laying out the beads required for the row or ticking off each repetition that make up a finished row. This stitch requires you to step-up after a row. This spot is usually clear because the beadwork will have an odd, gap-toothed look where the last bead of a row goes **(figure 2)**. When you stitch this bead in place you will sew through a bead in the previous row and the first bead of the row you have been stitching. As you step-up from row to row your starting point in a row will move diagonally along the beadwork. Occasionally I have missed the step-up spot and didn't discover my mistake until I'd gone all the way round again. It's irritating but the best thing you can do is pick out your stitching and sew in the skipped bead.

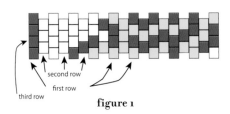

figure 1

Even-Count Flat Peyote

Even-count flat peyote is a flat piece of beadwork worked from side to side. It doesn't matter how many beads you start with so long as you start with an even number. Individual rows will always have the same number of beads and it might be an odd number or it might be an even number. The tail will end up in the first bead of the second row. Some people regard this stitch as the easiest form of peyote because you naturally step up to start a new row on both sides. Getting started can be a bit tricky. Just remember that the two principles apply: the first beads you picked up make up the first and second rows. The first bead you pick up for the third row will sit on top of the last bead in the first row and the bead you sew through, the one that could look as though it's in the same row is actually in the second row **(figure 3)**.

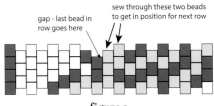

figure 2

Odd-Count Flat Peyote and Switching Needles

In this form of peyote, while you have a logical way to increase on one side, the other side requires a special turn to get the needle into position to start a new row. To avoid this problem, you'll be using a two-needle approach for the odd-count flat peyote projects in this book. Stretch and condition your thread as usual. Thread a needle onto each end. Set one needle aside — you only need to use one needle for a while. String a stop bead and slide it a couple of inches past the center of the thread. Pick up all the beads in the first two rows and center them between the two needles. Sew the first bead in the third row in place, using figure 3 as a guide. Sew the rest of the beads in the third row in place. When you pick up the last bead, pick it up as usual and slide it along the thread until it is next to the beadwork. Set the working needle aside and take up the other needle. Sew this needle through the last bead so that it is heading toward the beadwork **(figure 4)**. You will use this needle to sew the next two rows. Switch needles again after you finish the second of the next two rows and use the new needle for the next pair of rows. You'll keep switching needles like this after every two rows.

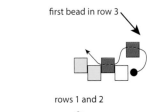

figure 3

To add thread always end on a row where you would normally switch needles — both needles will be on the same side at this point **(figure 5)**. Secure both threads by sewing back into the beadwork. Stretch and condition a comfortable length of new thread and thread a needle onto one end. String a stop bead and center it. Start in the center and sew through the beads in the last row and the next-to-last row until you sew through the last bead in the next-to-last row. Remove the stop bead and thread a needle. Stitch through beads to bring this needle through the last bead in the next-to-last row on the other side.

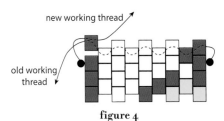

figure 4

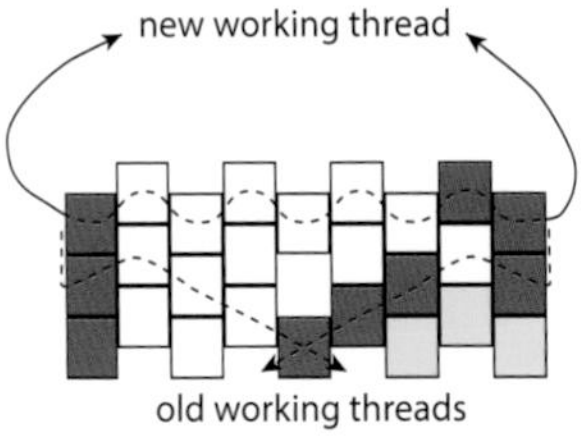

DIAGONAL PEYOTE

This flat peyote stitch gives you an angled piece of beadwork rather than a square or rectangle one **(figure 6)**. The stitch requires you to decrease along one side and increase along the other. The chart for each ornament will tell you what color beads you must pick up for the turns, but the principle is always the same for every turn. To decrease, you pick up an 11º or 15º seed bead or a cylinder bead. You then sew back

figure 5

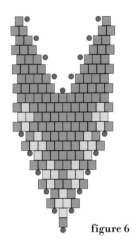

figure 6

These two beads will have a tendency to twist. Don't worry about it - you will lock them into position with the next row of peyote stitches.

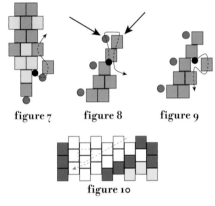

figure 7 figure 8 figure 9

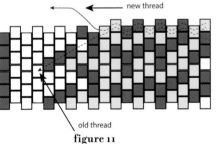

figure 10

new thread

old thread

figure 11

figure-8 knot

A

B

C

through a bead in the beadwork and continue normal peyote stitching **(figure 7)**. To increase, you pick up an 11º or 15º seed bead or cylinder bead and another bead. You then sew back though the first bead you picked up and pull it snugly against the beadwork **(figure 8)**. You then pick up another bead and resume normal peyote stitching **(figure 9)**. The stitch may seem a little confusing at first, but once you get the rhythm of it, diagonal peyote is quite straightforward. The 11º or 15º seed bead or cylinder bead on the increase side may twist out of position but you will fix that when you stitch back through it on the next row.

ADDING & ENDING THREAD — BEAD WEAVING

Peyote is forgiving because you can follow diagonal paths to start and end threads. Never trim excess thread if it is coming out of an edge bead. I have seen too many people trim the working thread by accident when they did this. Only trim an excess thread when it is coming out between two beads. You can secure a thread before you trim the excess or before you begin weaving with a new one **(figure 10, red line)**. Personally, I like to sew through several beads sewn with the old thread with the new thread again **(figure 11)**. These same principles apply to tubular, netted, and flat round as well as even- and one-needle odd-count.

Figure-8 Knots

In many of the ornaments, it's a good idea to tie at least one figure-8 knot before trimming the excess thread because the knot anchors the thread more securely. Pull the thread completely through a bead. Hold a loop to one side of the thread and sew underneath the thread between the beads. Twist the loop into a figure-8 and sew through the upper loop. Carefully tighten the knot so that it falls between the last bead you sewed through and the next bead. Sew through a few more beads and tie another knot if you choose. Otherwise, trim the thread. Always sew through a few beads after tying a knot and before trimming the excess thread. The needle in the photo is extra bendy because it is a twisted collapsible eye needle — your needle (I hope) is not going to be so distorted in shape.

BEAD EMBROIDERY

Materials and Tools

There are a variety of beading foundations available. I stitched these on Nicole's Bead Backing, but I also like to use Ultrasuede for a foundation. Both of these products are available in a variety of colors. Two other products you can use are Lacey's Stiff Stuff and Beadsmith's beading foundation. These only come in white and black, but you can dye the white to better coordinate with your project. Because of the range of colors these come in, I also think you're better off using a standard size D beading nylon thread rather than a braided or bonded thread.

Conventional practice recommends using E6000 adhesive to glue the finished beadwork to a backing. For dainty, little pieces like these ornaments I have found that a double-sided archival quality adhesive tape works very well — you can find this at most art and hobby supply stores.

Instead of the long needles used for beadweaving, you may find it easier to use short beading needles. Also, you will need a good pair of sharp fabric scissors to cut out and trim the beaded image as well as the backing. Have a pair of paper scissors handy to cut out the template.

STITCHES — BEAD EMBROIDERY

The basic stitch used for bead embroidery is a **backstitch**. For little pieces like these ornaments I pick up only two beads at a time **(figure 12, A)**, but it is more common to pick up three beads and sew back thorough the last bead for the backstitch **(figure**

12, B). Stretch and condition a comfortable length of thread. String a stop bead with an 8 in. (20cm) tail so that you can secure the thread later. Sew from the back to the front of your fabric. Pick up two beads. Sew straight down through the fabric and back up behind the second bead. Sew through it and pick up two beads. When a row when go exactly ow you want it to go sometimes the next row of stitching will nudge it into place. You can also sew through all the beads in a row again or stitch through a stubborn bead again. You will see in the directions a few references to stitching beads "on end". Pick up the beads one at a time and sew them in place so that you can see the holes when you look at the row from the side. Once the rows on either side of the on-end row are in place the beads in this row will stand up properly.

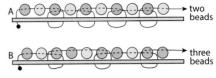

figure 12

ADDING & ENDING THREAD — EMBROIDERY

Rather than tying knots, secure your threads with a cross-hatch stitch. Secure old threads and attach new threads with this method: sew under a few stitches on the back of the piece. Choose a few other stitches and sew under them. Sew under the same stitches again a couple of times, and trim your thread (**figure 13, red line**).

figure 13

FINISHING WITH BRICK-STITCH EDGING

The finishing stitch used on these ornaments is a brick-stitch edging (**figure 14**). Start with a yard of thread and secure one end between the layers (**figure 15, a**). Sew through the beadwork layer. Pick up two beads and sew through both layers right next to the bead embroidery (**b**). Sew through the second bead again (**c**). Pick up another bead. Sew through both layers and the bead you just picked up (**d**). Continue stitching beads to edge with this stitch all around the piece. When you get back to the first bead, sew down through it rather than picking up a bead. Secure the thread and trim the excess. Because I am a big chicken, I usually don't trim the fabric as close to the beadwork as I should, so I go around the edge and push the edging beads onto the embroidery side of the ornament.

dashed line represents thread path
on wrong side of foundation

figure 14

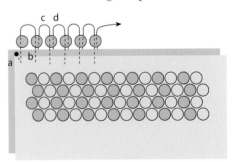

figure 15

WRAPPED LOOPS

You have to practice, practice, practice wrapped loops to learn to make them smoothly. Once you've gotten the technique down, you'll be wrapping loops without thinking about each micro-step. You will have to have a pair of chainnose pliers, a pair of roundnose pliers, and a pair of flush cutters to make wrapped loops. I also like to use a pair of 1mm pliers, but these are not essential.

Technique

First, string your beads and ornament part on a headpin as directed. Next, hold the headpin with 1mm pliers or the very tip of a pair of chainnose pliers against the beads—the pliers must touch the beads (**A**). Bend the wire (do not bend the tool) against the topside of the plier jaws at a 90-degree (right) angle. Set aside the pliers and note that there is a small space between the corner and the beads (**B**). Make a mark with a permanent marker on the roundnose pliers approximately ¼ in. (6mm) from the tips. Using the mark as a guide, place the bent headpin in the pliers so the beads hang down and the bend sticks out straight from the jaws like a cigar.

Going up and over the pliers, wrap the wire around only the upper jaw of the pliers (**C**). Look carefully at the wire in relation to the pliers — notice the gap between the beads and the bend as well as how the loop sticks out to the side (**D**). Switch the position of the partial loop so that it is around the lower jaw (**E**). You can do this either by turning the pliers over or by physically moving the headpin from the top jaw to the lower jaw. Make sure the partial loop is snugly on the pliers' jaw. Fix the image of a snowman in your mind: you want to end up with a round-ish circle centered over the beads. The straight bit of wire is like a scarf in a stiff breeze.

wrapped loops

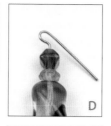

tassel making

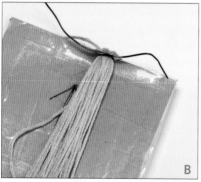

Now comes the hard part: Keep the wire on the pliers and alternate between pushing the corner against the pliers and sweeping the straight end across the corner. You want the wire to cross exactly over the corner so whatever you do, do not straighten out the corner **(F)**. Set aside the roundnose pliers. Hold the circle flat in a pair of chainnose pliers. Use your left hand to hold the chainnose pliers if you are right-handed and in your right hand if you are left-handed. Hold the end of the straight wire with the roundnose pliers in your dominant hand. Starting in the corner, wrap the wire around the bit between the corner and the beads and ornament **(G)**. Place each wrap next to the previous one, with no space showing between them. Stop wrapping when you meet the beads. Trim the excess wire with your flush cutters — always put the flat side of the cutter against the wraps **(H)**. Very little wire should stick out. If you have as much as 1/8 in. (3mm), get in there and trim again.

SAFETY TIP: Cover the wire when you are trimming the excess. These small bits can fly surprisingly far and are very dangerous if they hit you in the eye. You can also wear safety goggles. There will probably be a sharp nubbin sticking out no matter how closely you trim. Using chainnose pliers, gently guide this sharp tip into place next to the beads.

TASSEL MAKING

Materials and Tools

You can purchase tassels or sometimes recycle them from a scarf or the end of strand of semi-precious beads. However, they are easy to make and you can adapt this method to just about any size tassel. The basic thing to remember is that you want to be able to finish off the tassel by pulling the wire loop all the way up into the bead cap or cone you are using. This technique requires making a wrapped loop, so review the section above and make sure you have those tools on hand. You will also need an index card folded in half and taped together to keep it from flapping open. Finally, you will want a pair of good fabric scissors for cutting and trimming the fiber into a tassel. Have a 6-in. (15cm) piece of 22-gauge wire ready as well.

I usually use an entire skein of regular cotton embroidery floss, but you can use any similar fiber you like. Rayon has lovely colors, but it is slippery and difficult to work with. Silk can be nice to work with unless it is a fine, glossy thread. Bamboo thread is lovely, but you will probably only find it in specialty needlework shops.

Technique

First, unwind the embroidery skein and work out any snarls. Hold an end against the index card so that a little bit hangs below the bottom edge of the card. Start wrapping the floss around the card tightly, but not so tightly the card bows. Keep your floss pretty much centered on the card as you go. Wrap until you can't make another full wrap around the card — both ends must hang down from the same side of the card **(A)**. Slide the wire under all the threads and pull them sharply across each other, gathering up the threads as tightly as you can **(B)**. Using a chainnose pliers, bend one wire so that it points straight up from the threads. Pull the other wire around it, keeping the threads gathered up as tightly as possible. Continue wrapping the wire, but instead of wrapping it around the wire as in a wrapped loop, wrap so the wire lies on top of the thread **(C)**. Trim the excess wrapping wire, and insert the remaining wire through the hole in a cap or a cone. Finish the wrapped loop as above.

CHAPTER 1

Beginner Ornaments

RIBBON CANDY

This dainty little morsel is made with a variation of even-count flat peyote called two-drop. This means you treat two beads as if they were one: Instead of picking up a bead and sewing through a bead, you'll pick up two beads and sew through two beads. Consider making some candy to sweeten up a gift— you could even make it in someone's favorite colors.

NOTE Refer to even-count peyote, p. 9.

ORNAMENT

1 Stretch and condition 2 yd. (1.8m) of thread. Thread a needle, string on a stop bead, and slide it to 8 in. (20cm) from the end. Pick up a color A 11º seed bead, a color B 11º seed bead, a color C 11º seed bead, two As, a color D 11º seed bead, a color E 11º seed bead, and an A **(figure 1, a–b)**.

2 Pick up an A and an E, and sew through a D and an A **(b–c)**. Continue picking up two beads and sewing through two beads. Since the colors run in straight lines through the beadwork, a bead will always sit on top of a bead of the same color **(figure 2)**. Repeat until the beadwork is approximately 8 in. (20cm) long. You can make it a little longer if you like, but don't make it shorter.

3 Leave your needle on the working thread, and thread a new needle onto the tail. Fold the end over ½ in. (1.3cm), and sew it in place, going from one side to the other. Secure the thread in the short folded end, not the long body of the beadwork, and trim.

4 Fold over the other end of the bead-work ½ in. Make sure that this fold is not on the same side of the beadwork as the first fold. Take up the working thread needle again, and sew this end in place. Work your needle back to the center of the beadwork, and come through an A in the center wide stripe that is next to the folded end. Pick up eight 15º seed beads, and sew through an A on the

other side of the stripe. Choose a bead that is as close to the folded end as possible. Jam the needle through the beadwork, getting it to come through as close as possible to the fold end on the other side **(photo)**. Sew through a few of the As in the center stripe, and jam the needle back through to the loop side. Sew through the loop again, and secure the thread. Trim.

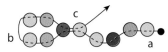

figure 1

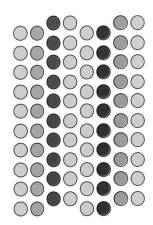

figure 2

Supplies

- 11º seed beads

  - **3g** color A (silver-lined crystal AB)

  - **1g** color B (silver-lined medium pink)

  - **1g** color C (silver-lined light siam)

  - **1g** color D (silver-lined medium emerald)

  - **1g** color E (silver-lined mint green)

- **8** 15º seed beads (silver-lined crystal)

- Size D or equivalent beading thread

- Size 10 beading needles

- Stop bead

- Conditioner

- Ruler

- Thread snips

○ 11º seed beads, color A

◔ 11º seed beads, color B

● 11º seed beads, color C

● 11º seed beads, color D

○ 11º seed beads, color E

"PAPER" CHAIN

Remember making paper chains? Even though we all had the same construction paper, everyone's chains looked different. As you can see, I've gone for the classic kindergarten approach of using every color I could find. You can take a classier approach and choose just a handful of coordinating colors. This would be a great project for a beading group to work on together and donate to a shelter or some other charity.

Supplies

- 11° seed beads in assorted colors of your choice (each solid color link requires approximately **2.5g** of beads)
- Size D or equivalent beading thread
- Size 10 beading needles
- Stop beads
- Conditioner
- Ruler
- Thread snips

TIP: If you want a daintier chain, start with four beads rather than six and make the strips a little shorter than recommended for the six-count strips. You can also use a flat peyote chart to develop a pattern other than length-wise stripes.

NOTE Review the pointers for even-count peyote, p. 9 and securing threads on, p. 10.

CHAIN

NOTE The sample chain has 36 links and each link is made from a strip about 3 in. (7.6cm) long. The completed chain is just over 1 yd. (.9m) long. Your finished chain will vary, depending up how long each of your links actually is and how many links you make. If you have a small tree, it might be fun to make lots of individual links or even mini chains of only two or three links.

1 Stretch and condition 2 yd. (1.8m) of thread. String a stop bead, and slide it to 6 in. (15cm) from the end of the thread. Pick up six 11° seed beads, then start sewing even-count peyote rows with the same color beads **(figure 1)**. Keep going until the peyote strip is approximately 3 in. (7.6cm) long.

2 Make sure the ends will fit together as shown in **figure 2**. Sew through the beads that are sticking out, going from one side to the other. If this is the first time you have worked with peyote, this is called "zipping up." Sew back through the beads again. Secure the thread, and trim. Remove the stop bead, and end the tail.

3 Keep making links. For the second and every subsequent link, pass the strip through a finished link before zipping it together. All is not lost if you should forget—just pass the next link through two links before zipping it together.

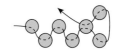

figure 1

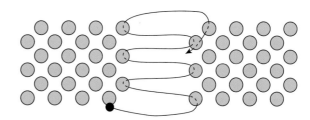

figure 2

up close!

CLASSIC BOW

No package is complete without a bow, so think about dressing up a gift such as a bottle of wine, olive oil, or some homemade holiday treats with one of these bows. Personalize it by making it in someone's favorite colors. Of course, it makes a lovely gift all by itself.

NOTE Review even-count peyote, p. 9, and securing thread, p. 10.

ORNAMENT

1 Stretch and condition 2 yd. (1.8m) of thread. String a stop bead, and slide it to 8 in. (20cm) from the end. Pick up a color A 11º seed bead, a color B 11º seed bead, two As, a B, and an A **(figure 1)**. These beads form your first two rows. Slide them down to the stop bead.

2 The pick-up pattern for every row is A, A, B. Begin sewing peyote stitches, and continue until you have a strip 4½ in. (11.4cm) long. Make sure the ends will zip together before moving to the next step **(figure 2)**. Arrange the beadwork as shown in the **photo**, and zip the ends together. End the threads.

3 Stretch and condition 1 yd. (.9m) of thread. String a stop bead, and slide it 12 in. (30cm) from the end of the thread. Pick up the beads in the same order you picked them up in step 1, and work in even-count peyote stitch until you have a strip 1–1¼ in. (2.5–3.2cm) long. (The white sample was made with the longer measurement, and the red and green bow with the shorter.) Follow the thread path shown in **figure 3** to make the first decrease turn. Work two two-bead rows, a decrease turn, and two one-bead rows. End with a point **(figure 4)**. Secure and trim the working thread. Leave the tail intact. Make a second strip the same size as the first one. Remove the stop beads, and sew each strip to the bow loop. Use **figure 5** as a guide for positioning the strips. Make sure the angle between the two strips allows space for the "knot." Secure the threads in the strips.

4 Stretch and condition 1½ yd. (1.4m) of thread. String on a stop bead, and slide it to 6 in. (15cm) from the end. Work in even-count peyote stitch to make another strip using the same pattern. Stop when it is 1⅜ in. (3.5cm) long. Check to make sure it will zip together. Hold it around the bow, and zip the ends of the strip together. Ideally, it will fit snugly, but not so snugly you have to fight to zip it together. Secure the thread and tail. Trim the excess threads. Feed a ribbon under this strip to hang.

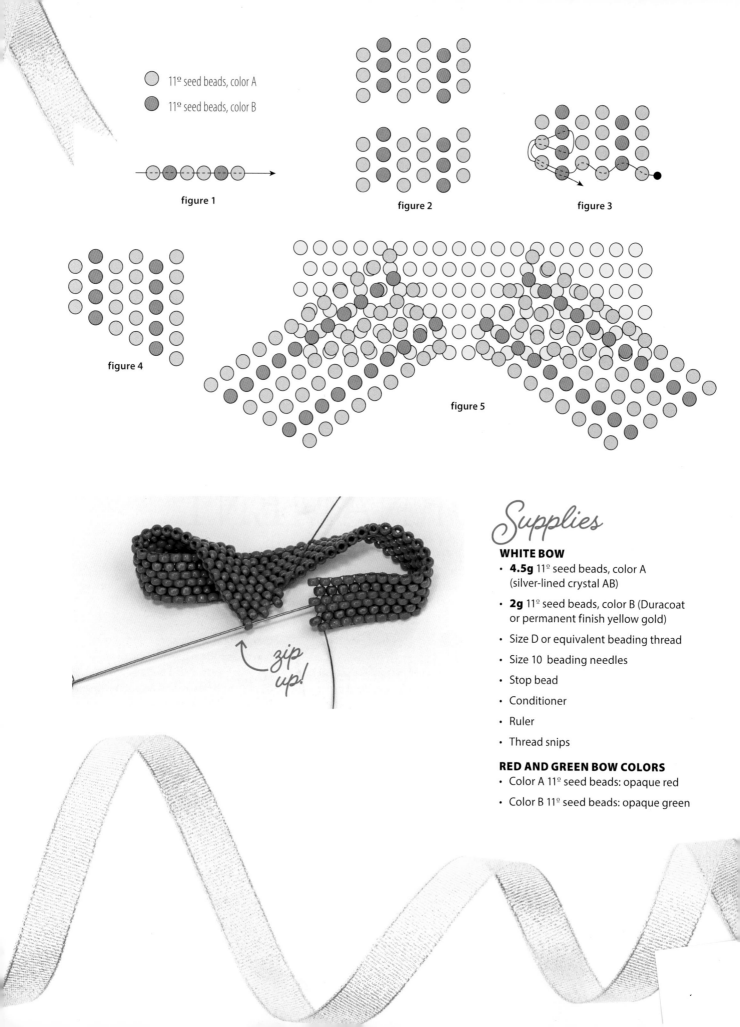

○ 11º seed beads, color A
● 11º seed beads, color B

figure 1

figure 2

figure 3

figure 4

figure 5

zip up!

Supplies

WHITE BOW

- **4.5g** 11º seed beads, color A (silver-lined crystal AB)
- **2g** 11º seed beads, color B (Duracoat or permanent finish yellow gold)
- Size D or equivalent beading thread
- Size 10 beading needles
- Stop bead
- Conditioner
- Ruler
- Thread snips

RED AND GREEN BOW COLORS

- Color A 11º seed beads: opaque red
- Color B 11º seed beads: opaque green

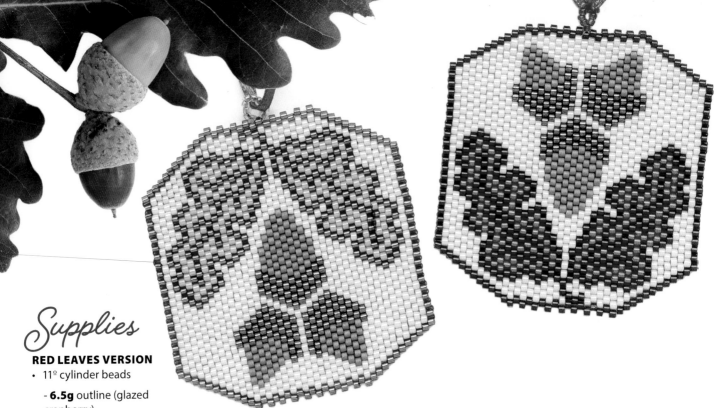

Supplies

RED LEAVES VERSION

- 11º cylinder beads

  - **6.5g** outline (glazed cranberry)

  - **1.5g** leaf filler (silver-lined brick red)

  - **1.5g** acorn body (matte medium beige)

  - **1g** acorn cap (dark bronze)

  - **3g** background (ceylon ivory)

- **10** or **11** 15º seed beads (semi matte silver-lined light siam)

- Size D or equivalent beading thread

- Sizes 10 and 12 beading needles

- Stop bead

- Conditioner

- Thread snips

GREEN LEAVES VERSION COLORS

- Outline: silver-lined pine green cylinder beads

- Leaf filler: ceylon mint green cylinder beads

- Acorn body: matte medium beige cylinder beads

- Acorn cap: dark bronze cylinder beads

- Background: ceylon ivory cylinder beads

- 15º seed beads: semi-matte lime-lined crystal AB

OAK LEAF ORNAMENT

This ornament can decorate more than a tree. Consider tying it with a ribbon to a candlestick on a table set for a holiday meal. Do you know an avid reader? Perhaps they would appreciate an oak leaf bookmark! Choose between two colorways to evoke autumn or look forward to spring.

NOTE Refer to odd-count flat peyote guidelines for switching needles, p. 9 and adding thread on p. 10. You'll start at the bottom of the wide portion with the two rows that are outlined in red and work toward the leaves. Finish the panel by working the decreasing rows on one end and then the decreasing rows on the other end.

Work from the chart. Some people like to lay out each row of beads as they go; some people prefer to tick off each bead on the chart as they go. Rather than marking up your book, you can make a copy of the chart.

ORNAMENT

1 Stretch and condition 2 yd. (1.8m) of thread. Thread a needle onto each end. Pick up an outline bead, 10 background beads, seven body beads, two cap beads, a background bead, two cap beads, seven body beads, 10 background beads, and an outline bead. Center the beads between the needles. Pick up another outline bead, and begin working in peyote stitch, following the **pattern (figure 1)**. When you reach the other side, refer to "switching needles," p. 9.

2 Continue working rows following the pattern. It will be necessary to add thread at some point. Refer to instructions for adding thread for odd-count peyote, p. 9.

3 When you reach the point where the rows begin decreasing in length, follow the thread path shown by the red line in **figure 2** to get set up to sew the next row.

4 You can put the loop on either the acorn side or the leaf side of the ornament. Bring a thread through the center edge bead in whichever side you chose. If you started a new thread, start weaving from somewhere in the body until you make it through the center bead **(figure 3)**. To sew a loop on the leaf side, pick up 10 15º seed beads. Sew back through the center bead and all of the beads in the loop again to strengthen and tighten it **(figure 4)**. Secure the thread in the body of the ornament, and end the thread. To sew a loop on the acorn side, pick up 11 15ºs, and sew back through the first 15º and the center bead **(figure 5)**. Sew through all of the beads again to tighten and strengthen the loop. Secure the thread in the body of the ornament, and end the threads.

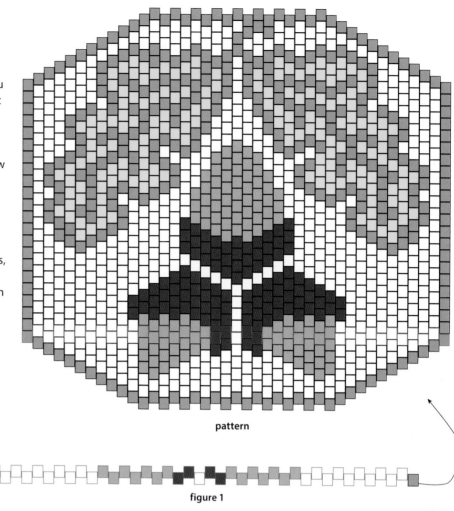

pattern

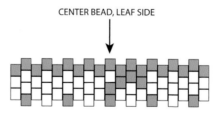

figure 1

figure 2

- ▣ 11º cylinder beads, acorn body
- ◼ 11º cylinder beads, acorn cap
- ▨ 11º cylinder beads, outline
- ▨ 11º cylinder beads, leaf filler
- ☐ 11º cylinder beads, background
- ● 15º seed beads

CENTER BEAD, LEAF SIDE

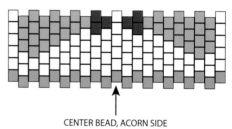

CENTER BEAD, ACORN SIDE

figure 3

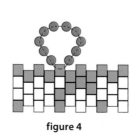

figure 4

figure 5

19

CANDY CANE

Is a tree really complete without candy canes? As a child I never liked candy canes all that much because I'm not fond of peppermint. But now they come in all sorts of exotic flavors! Take a cue from the mango-banana flavored example (shown below) and come up with your own flavor blends.

NOTE Tubular odd-count peyote flies in the face of reason and does not require step-ups after each row. In fact, once you get going, it sews as if it were one long continuous row. You may find it helpful to use a toothpick as a form until the piece of beadwork is long enough to easily hold. Refer to "Wrapped Loops," p. 11.

ORNAMENT

1 Stretch and condition 2 yd. (1.8m) of thread. Pick up two color A 11º seed beads, two color B 11º seed beads, two As, and one B. Sew through all the beads again **(figure 1)**.

2 Pick up a B, skip an A, and sew through an A **(figure 2, a–b)**. Pick up an A, skip the next B, and sew through a B **(b–c)**. Pick up a B, skip the next A, and sew through an A **(c–d)**. Pick up an A, skip a B, and sew through a B **(d–e)**. Notice that this is the first B added, although you will not see this as you stitch.

3 Continue working in peyote stitch until your tube is about 4 in. (10cm) long. Always pick up whatever color of bead you just sewed through, and your diagonals will develop nicely. Close the end by sewing together three or four beads that stick out the most **(figure 3)**.

4 Fold the piece of wire in half. Slide a bead of either color into the fold. Feed the wire ends through the tube, and pull the bead tightly against the tube. Treating both wires as one, make a very small wrapped loop (see "Wrapped Loops," p. 11). Cut the ribbon into four equal pieces. Feed two through the loop, and tie them in place with a knot. Use the other two to tie a bow over the wraps. Shape the tube into a cane shape.

Supplies

PEPPERMINT

- **2g** 11º seed beads, color A (opaque red)
- **2g** 11º seed beads, color B (opaque white)
- **12 in. (30cm)** 24-gauge wire
- **4 ft. (1.22m)** ¼-in. (6mm) ribbon
- Size D or equivalent beading thread
- Size 10 beading needles
- Conditioner
- Thread snips
- Roundnose pliers
- Chainnose pliers
- Flush cutters

MANGO-BANANA COLORS

- Color A 11º seed beads: opaque orange
- Color B 11º seed beads: opaque yellow

○ 11º seed bead, color A
○ 11º seed bead, color B

figure 1

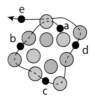

figure 2

figure 3

mango banana

CHAPTER 2
Advanced Beginner Ornaments

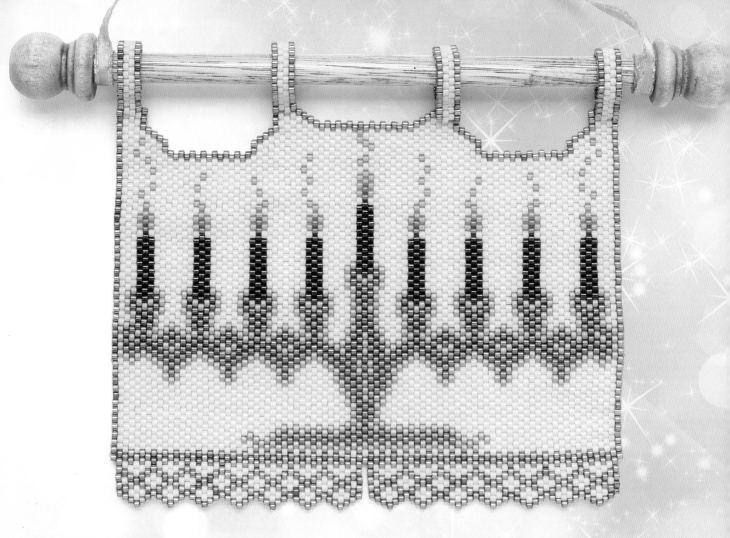

Supplies

- 11º cylinder beads
  - **1.75g** color A (metallic golden olive iris)
  - **14g** color B (matte white)
  - **2.5g** color C (matte gold)
  - **2.75g** color D (light bronze)
  - **1.25g** color E (opaque cobalt luster)
  - **1.25g** color F (silver-lined orange)
  - **.5g** color G (silver-lined red-orange)
- **1** ¼-in. (6mm) dowel, 5½" (14cm) long
- **2** wooden decorative end caps to fit dowel
- Wood stain
- Ribbon or embroidery floss to make a hanger
- Wood glue
- Size D or equivalent beading thread
- Size 10 beading needles
- Stop beads
- Conditioner
- Thread snips

MENORAH WALL HANGING

Participating in lighting a menorah during Hanukkah or even a Shabbat candle on Friday night in a Jewish home is a wonderful experience. I was 13 the first time I was invited to join a friend's family on a Friday night and I have never forgotten the atmosphere of quiet spirituality. Over the years I've been present when many candles and menorahs were lit and every time I revisit that moment.

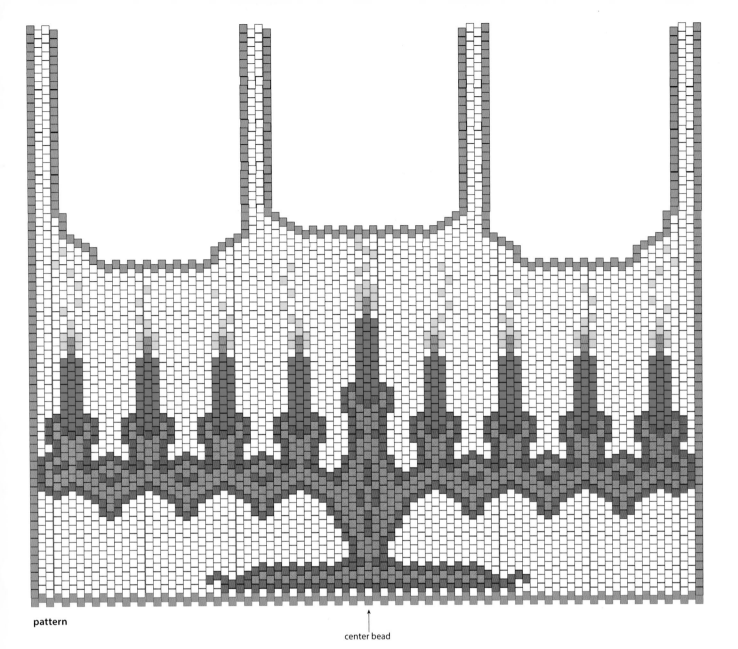

pattern

center bead

■ 11º cylinder bead, color A

□ 11º cylinder bead, color B

■ 11º cylinder bead, color C

▨ 11º cylinder bead, color D

■ 11º cylinder bead, color E

▨ 11º cylinder bead, color F

□ 11º cylinder bead, color G

NOTE Review the instructions for odd-count flat peyote, p. 9, especially the section on adding thread. When you get to the straps, refer to the section on even-count peyote on p. 9. You'll start at the bottom with the two rows that are outlined in red and continue working toward the candles. Work from the chart. Some people like to lay out each row of beads as they go; some people prefer to tick off each bead on the chart as they go. Rather than marking up your book, make a copy of the chart.

WALL HANGING

1 Stain the dowel and end caps and set them aside to dry while you stitch the wall hanging. You will probably want to use more than one coat of stain. Allow

it to dry completely before applying another coat. When you like the depth of color from the stain, glue one end cap to the dowel.

2 Stretch and condition 2 yd. (1.8m) of thread. String on a stop bead and center it. Pick up 89 color A 11º cylinder beads, and center them on the thread, adjusting the stop bead to do so.

3 Pick up another A, and begin working in peyote stitch. Aside from the first and last beads in this third row, all of the beads will be color B 11º cylinder beads. After you finish this row, remove the stop bead. Follow the guidelines on switching needles, p. 9. Follow the **pattern** from here.

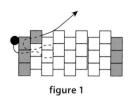

figure 1

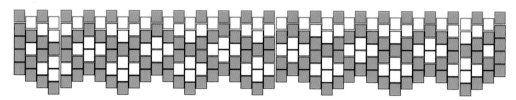

figure 2

4 Continue working in peyote stitch, adding and ending thread as needed (see p. 10). When you reach the top where the decreases begin, first stitch the wide middle section and complete one strap. Refer to **figure 1** to work the decrease turns. Add thread with a single needle to sew the two outer straps and the remaining inner strap. Trim any excess tail threads, but do not trim the working threads. You will need them in the next step.

5 Sew the beads in the last two rows of the straps to the beads outlined in red at the base of the straps. Make sure you sew them all to the same side of the wall hanging. Secure each thread as you go and trim the excess.

6 Stretch and condition 2 yd. (1.8m) of thread. Note that for these bottom panels you will read the chart from top to bottom. Thread a needle onto each end. Pick up 22 As and 21 Bs in an alternating pattern as shown by the two long rows of beads outlined in red **(figure 2)**. Center them between the needles. Pick up another A, and begin working in two-needle odd-count peyote stitch. Continue working eight rows following the pattern in **figure 2**. For the final two rows, you do not have to decrease to sew the points. Sew through As along the edge to get in position to work on the next point. Refer to **figure 1** when turning around on the sides. Secure all threads in the body of the panel — do not use the first two rows of A and B beads for securing your thread or tail. Trim the excess threads. Make a second panel.

7 Stretch and condition 18 in. (46cm) of thread. String a stop bead and center it. Sew through the center bead at the bottom of the menorah as indicated by the arrow in the **pattern** (see p.23). Zip one panel in place and secure the thread. Trim the excess. Remove the stop bead, and thread a needle onto the thread. Zip the second panel in place. End the thread.

8 Slide the dowel through the loops, and glue the second end cap in place. Allow it to dry thoroughly before tying on a ribbon or embroidery thread for the hanger.

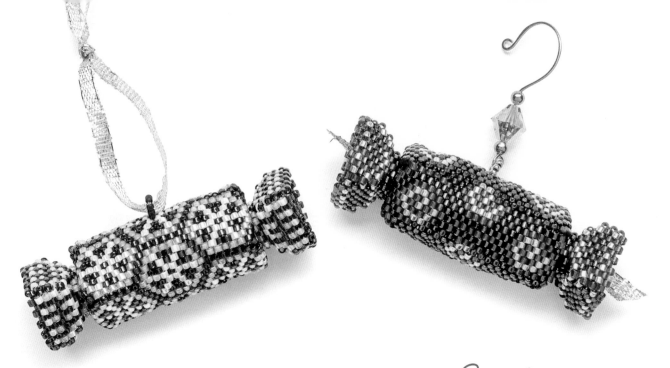

WRAPPED SWEETIE

I have a terrible sweet tooth, so I always look forward to the special candies and baked goods that appear during the holidays. The sight of a biscuit tin or a plate wrapped in cellophane is a sure sign that there is something tasty in that gift. Not everyone appreciates being inundated with mountains of sweets, so I made this little sweetie because no one can object to some eye candy.

NOTE Review the section on stepping up in even-count tubular peyote and the section on adding thread on page 10. As with any patterned peyote project, you may prefer to print a copy of the pattern and mark that up rather than marking up your book. Often tubular peyote is stitched around a form. I found that your finger works pretty well as a form for the sweetie.

ORNAMENT

1 Familiarize yourself with the **pattern** for the sweetie you have chosen. Note the beads that are outlined in blue and yellow. The ones outlined in yellow running in a jagged line along the bottom of the chart are the two starting rows. The diagonal blue outlined line is the step-up row. Take note of the two rows that have a square with a blue outline on the upper right-hand side of the chart. Even though the diagonal line runs from right to left and from bottom to top, these are the last two rows you'll work in regular peyote stitch in the chart. If you made a copy of the chart, line up the sides and you can see why the diagonal line jumps from

Supplies

SPIRAL SWEETIE
- 11º cylinder beads
  - **3.5g** color A (silver-lined brick red)
  - **2.75g** color B (silver-lined spruce green)
  - **1.25g** color C (gold)
- **8** 15º seed beads (gold)
- Size D or equivalent beading thread
- Size 10 and 12 beading needles
- Stop beads
- Conditioner
- Thread snips
- Optional: 2 6mm gold square spacer beads with 1.5mm holes, 18 in. (46cm) of ribbon, and toothpick or awl

SNOWFLAKE SWEETIE COLORS
- 11º cylinder beads
  - color A: silver-lined cobalt
  - color B: luminous ocean blue
  - color C: white pearl ceylon
- 15º seed beads: matte transparent cobalt

pattern 1

the body of the ornament. Stretch and condition 1 yd. (.9m) of thread. Secure it in the body of the sweetie, and then complete the points on this side of the ornament. If your thread is long enough, sew through one of the points to exit the A at the tip. You should now have a thread on each end of the sweetie exiting a point. You'll finish one side of the sweetie, and then the other.

4 At one end, pick up a B, an A, and a B, and sew through the next point bead **(figure 2)**. Repeat a total of four times. Draw the points together so the beads form a ring. Sew through another B, A, B, and A. The last A will be a point bead.

5 Pick up a B, and sew through the next A. Repeat around the circle, and step up through a B **(figure 3)**. Pick up an A, and sew through a B. Pick up two Bs, and sew through a B. Repeat these stitches around the circle, and step up through the first A and three Bs **(figure 4)**. Pick up an A, and sew through an A. Pick up an A, and sew through two Bs. Repeat these stitches around the edge. Step up through the first A **(figure 5)**.

pattern 2

the left side to the right side. Stretch and condition a comfortable length of thread. String a stop bead, and slide it to 8 in. (20cm) from the end.

2 **Spiral Sweetie:** Pick up this sequence four times: two color A 11º cylinder beads, two color B 11º cylinder beads, three As, two Bs, and an A. Sew through all the beads again, and step up through the first A (look for the tail). Pick up a B (marked with a blue outline and an X in the chart), and begin working in peyote stitch **(pattern 1)**.
Snowflake Sweetie: Pick up this sequence four times: two As, two Bs, an A, a color C 11º cylinder bead, an A, two

Bs, and an A. Step up through the first A (look for the tail). Pick up a B (marked with a blue outline and an X in the pattern), and begin working in peyote stitch **(pattern 2)**.

3 Follow the chart. When you get to the points at the top, sew through the As along the edge to get in position for the next row or to continue a row **(figure 1)**. If your thread is still long enough, sew through one of the points to exit the A at the tip and then set it aside for now. If it is short, end the thread in the body of the ornament (not in the outside edge of As). Remove the stop bead, and secure the tail in

6 Pick up a C, and sew through the next A. Pick up an A, a B, and an A, and sew through an A. Repeat around the circle, and step up through a C **(figure 6)**. Pick up a C, and sew through an A. Pick up two Cs, and sew through an A. Pick up a C, and sew through a C. Repeat along the circle, and step up through the first C **(figure 7)**.

7 Pick up an A, and sew through a C. Continue picking up As and sewing through Cs all around the circle. Step up through an A **(figure 8)**. Pick up a B, and sew through an A. Continue picking up Bs and sewing through As all around the circle. Step up through a B (not shown).

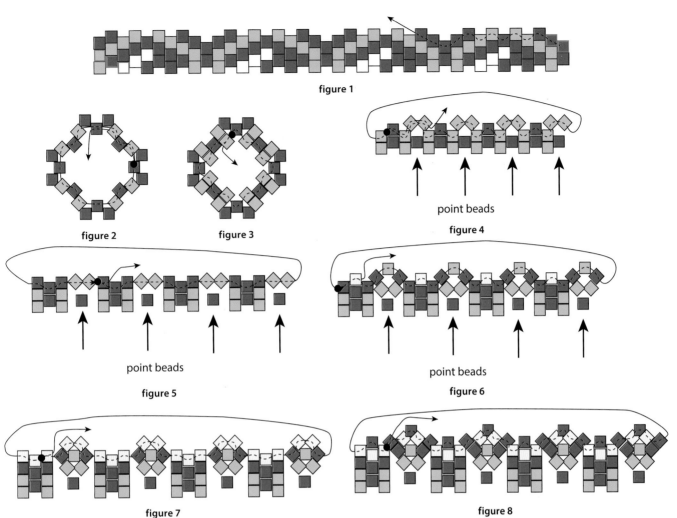

figure 1

figure 2

figure 3

point beads

figure 4

point beads

figure 5

point beads

figure 6

figure 7

figure 8

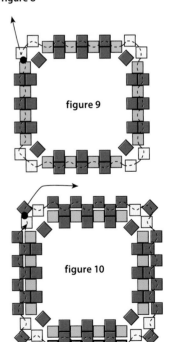

figure 9

figure 10

8 Pick up two Cs, and sew through a B. Pick up an A, and sew through a B. Pick up an A, and sew through a B. Pick up an A, and sew through a B. Repeat around the circle. Step up through a C **(figure 9)**. Pick up an A, and sew through a C. Pick up an A, and sew through an A. Pick up an A, and sew through an A. Pick up an A, and sew through an A. Pick up an A, and sew through a C. Continue picking up As and sewing them in around the circle. Step up through an A **(figure 10)**.

9 Work a row of peyote stitches, picking up only Bs. Step up through a B. Work a row of peyote stitches using only As. Step up through an A. Work a row of peyote stitches using only Cs. Step up through a C. Work two rows of peyote stitches using only As. Step up through an A. End the thread.

10 Repeat steps 4–9 at the other end to finish the wrapper. Stretch and condition 12 in. (30cm) of thread. Secure it in the body of the ornament, and bring your needle through one of the Cs (spiral sweetie) or As (snowflake sweetie) in the middle row that is marked with an X on the pattern. Pick up eight 15º seed beads, and sew through the C or A again to form a circle. Sew through all these beads again a couple of times to tighten and strengthen the loop. End the thread.

11 Optional: Double up the ribbon and tie the ends in a knot a couple of inches from the end. Feed the other end through one of the spacer beads. Feed the ribbon through the ornament and then through the second spacer bead. Tie a knot to hold the bead in place against the ornament—use a toothpick or an awl to help coax the knot into position.

CARDINAL

There is nothing quite like seeing that flash of red made by a cardinal in flight on a snowy day. When I was a child, our neighbors always made sure sunflower seeds were available all winter for the cardinals because they loved these cheeky birds. They also thought it was good luck to see one on Christmas, so I think they wanted to make sure that they would see at least one.

NOTE Review the techniques for bead embroidery on p. 10. Also, if you are using Ultrasuede you may find it easier to transfer the outline details with tailor's chalk. If you are using Ultrasuede for both the foundation and the backing, I recommend including a piece of Stiff Stuff or Beadsmith's beading foundation between the two layers. In step 6, cut one piece of Stiff Stuff or foundation slightly smaller than the beaded fabric. Tape or glue this to the back of the beadwork, and allow it to dry if you glued it. Then proceed.

ORNAMENT

1 Trace or copy the **pattern**. Cut it out and trace it onto your beading foundation. If you are using a white foundation, use a magic marker to color it so it blends better with the beads. (I tried dying it with hibiscus tea with limited success.) Do not cut the bird out of the foundation yet. Refer to the pattern to sketch in the lines showing the different color blocks.

2 Stretch and condition a comfortable length of thread. Sew through the foundation from back to front where the

bird's eye goes. Leave a 6-in. (15cm) tail. Sew the 8° seed bead eye in place with the hole showing — you will have to sew through the bead at least twice to make it lie flat. Tie the thread and tail together next to the foundation.

3 Fill in the face with the color A 11° seed beads (jet). Outline where it runs alongside the red, then outline the throat and beak. Fill in with rows that run parallel to the throat. Next, fill in the

crest with color B 11º seed beads (luster cherry red). Start by stitching a row that runs from the beak to the tip of the crest. Continue filling with rows that run parallel to the first crest row.

4 Stitch the wings with color C 11º seed beads (opaque pepper red or maroon). Outline the wing along the inside and outside — do not run a row parallel to the crest beads. Stitch one row next to the inside outline. Fill in the rest, working from the outside in toward the two rows next to the belly.

5 Outline the outer belly with color D 11º seed beads (opaque red). Fill in with rows that run from the outline to the wings. Stitch a 12-bead row of Cs down the center of the tail. Change direction and stitch a few rows of only two or three beads at the base of this line. Stitch a couple of rows of Bs on each side of this line. Fill in the beak with color E 11º seed beads (burnt orange-lined jonquil). Secure this thread and trim the excess.

6 Trim the beaded foundation to about a bead's width away from your stitching. Stretch and condition 2 yd. (1.8m) of thread, and secure it near the tip of the crest. Tape or glue the bird onto bead backing or Ultrasuede. Avoid the edges of the beaded shape. Allow the glue to dry, and trim this piece to the same size or slightly larger than the beaded shape. Be careful not to trim the thread!

7 Refer to "Finishing with brick-stitch edging," p. 11, and sew the fabrics together with this stitch. Use Fs for the edging. Don't forget to stitch the first and last brick-stitched beads together. After you have sewn the last stitch, sew through the beadwork to exit near the tip of the crest making sure you are exiting the fabric and not a bead. Pick up 15 15º seed beads, and sew through the fabric a couple of stitches from where you picked up the 15ºs. The loop should straddle the tip of the crest. Sew through the 15ºs again a couple of times, and secure your thread. Trim the excess.

Supplies

- **1** 8º seed bead (jet black)
- 11º seed beads
  - **.5g** color A (jet black)
  - **1.75g** color B (luster cherry red)
  - **2.5g** color C (opaque pepper red or maroon)
  - **2.5g** color D (opaque red)
  - **1g** color E (burnt orange-lined jonquil)
  - **2g** color F (malachite green iris)
- **15** 15º seed beads (gold)
- Bead backing, Ultrasuede, Stiff Stuff or Beadsmith's beading foundation for stitching
- Bead backing or Ultrasuede for a backing
- Size D or equivalent nylon beading thread
- Short size 11 or 12 beading needles
- Conditioner
- Thread snips
- Paper and fabric scissors
- Pencil and/or tailor's chalk
- Glue or double-sided archival tape
- Tracing paper or access to a copy machine

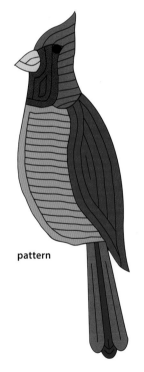

pattern

● 8º seed bead

● 11º seed bead, color A

● 11º seed bead, color B

● 11º seed bead, color C

● 11º seed bead, color D

○ 11º seed bead, color E

PARTRIDGE

"The Twelve Days of Christmas" is an odd song full of improbable gifts.
It sure is fun to sing, though, especially the "fiiiiiive golden rings" part.
However, anyone lucky enough to receive this partridge ornament as a gift
is unlikely to find anything peculiar about it at all.

NOTE Review the techniques for bead embroidery on p. 10. Take note of the section explaining what stitching or sewing 'edgewise' means. Also, if you are using Ultrasuede, you may find it easier to transfer the outline details with tailor's chalk. If you are using two pieces of Ultrasuede, I recommend you include a piece of Stiff Stuff or Beadsmith's beading foundation between the two layers. When you get to step 7, cut a piece of either of these foundations that is slightly smaller than the beaded fabric. Tape or glue this to the back of the beadwork and allow it to dry if you glued it. Then proceed with step 7.

ORNAMENT

1 Trace or copy the **pattern**. Cut it out, and trace it onto your beading foundation. If you are using a white foundation, you can use a magic marker or dye it with black tea or coffee to color it so it blends better with the beads. Refer to the pattern to sketch the lines showing the different color or pattern blocks. Do not cut the bird out of the foundation yet.

2 Stretch and condition a comfortable length of thread. Sew through the foundation from back to front where the eye goes. Leave a 6-in. (15cm) tail. Sew the 8° seed bead eye in place with the hole showing. You will have to use at least two stitches to make sure it lies in place properly. Tie the thread and tail together next to the foundation.

3 Use four color H 11° seed beads to sew the orange line in place. These beads go edgewise, so sew them in place, one at a time **(figure)**. Continue the line with backstitched color C 11° seed beads. Sew through the Cs again to smooth the line. Backstitch a row of color D 11° seed beads right in front of the eye beads to mark the beak. End this line at the throat with a C. Fill In the area in front of the H and C line with more Ds. Follow the shape of the H and C line, working from the line to the edge of the foundation. Include one C next to the one in the beak line.

4 Keep working in backstitch, and fill in the area on the other side of the

line with color A 11° seed beads. Work from the outside of the shape to the inside. There may be a slightly bald area up near the back of the bird's neck. You can fill this in with a line of beads sewn edgewise.

5 Scatter groups of two or three As along the back and tail. Avoid the belly. Partially outline these scattered As with scallops using the color F 11° seed beads. Fill in the scallops with color E 11° seed beads. At the same time, outline the back and tail of the bird with backstitched Es.

6 Fill in the front of the belly with alternating backstitched rows of Cs and color G 11° seed beads. Fill in the back belly with Ds. Fill in the beak with the Hs in tapering rows of backstitched beads. End with one bead at the tip of the beak.

7 Trim the foundation about a bead's width from the beadwork. Stretch and condition 2 yd. (1.8m) of thread. Secure the thread on the wrong side near the middle of the bird's back, and

Supplies

- **1** 8º seed bead (opaque brown)
- 11º seed beads
  - **2g** color A (silver gray ceylon)
  - **1.5g** color B (metallic gold iris)
  - **1.25g** color C (black opaque)
  - **1.25g** color D (light gray-lined topaz)
  - **1.25g** color E (metallic brown iris)
  - **1.25g** color F (matte metallic brown iris)
  - **1g** color G (opaque white 11º seed beads)
  - **.5g** color H (matte opaque vermillion red AB)
- **12** 15º seed beads (gold)
- Bead backing, Ultrasuede, Stiff Stuff, or Beadsmith's beading foundation for stitching
- Bead backing or Ultrasuede for backing the ornament
- Size D or equivalent beading thread
- Short size 11 or 12 beading needles
- Conditioner
- Thread snips
- Tracing paper or access to a copy machine
- Paper and fabric scissors
- Pencil or tailor's chalk
- Glue or double-sided archival tape

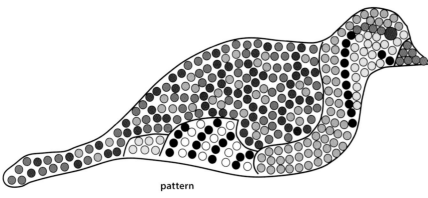

pattern

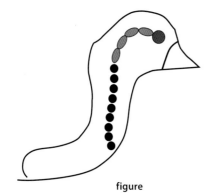

figure

●	8º seed bead
○	11º seed bead, color A
●	11º seed bead, color C
○	11º seed bead, color D
●	11º seed bead, color E
●	11º seed bead, color F
○	11º seed bead, color G
⬭ ●	11º seed bead, color H (shown edgewise)

keep it out of the way while you prepare the bird for finishing. Tape or glue the bird onto bead backing or Ultrasuede. Avoid the edges of the beaded shape. Allow the glue to dry, and trim this piece to the same size or slightly larger than the beaded shape. Be careful not to trim the thread!

8 Refer to "Finishing with brick-stitch edging," p. 11. Starting at the top center of the back, sew the fabrics together with this stitch. Use the color B metallic gold iris beads for the edging. Don't forget to stitch the first and last brickstitched beads together. After you have sewn the last stitch, make sure you are coming out of fabric and not a bead. Pick up 12 15º seed beads, and sew through the fabric a couple of stitches from where you picked up the 15ºs. Sew through the 15ºs again a couple of times, and end the thread.

FANTASY SWAGS

Branching fringe is an old — and
I believe — undervalued technique.
It's forgiving, it's versatile, and it's
incredibly easy to give a swag your
own personal touch, especially with
your choice of turn-around beads at
the end of every branch and trunk.
You can use any colors you like to
create your own unique fantasy swag.

NOTE Every swag has a main trunk
**(figure 1, blue beads with red out-
lines)**. When the directions say "up," that
means you stitch towards the decorative
bead at the top. "Down" means that
you stitch towards the end where the
turn-around bead(s) are **(various shapes
with green outlines)**. Branches **(black
outlines)** come off the trunk. When you
are stitching a branch "up" means that you
are stitching towards the trunk. "Down"
means that you are working towards the
branch's turn-around bead(s). It is possible
for a branch to have branches. The same
principles apply: "up" means you are stitching towards a branch or even a trunk and
"down" means you are stitching towards a
turn-around.

This is a very forgiving project. If you find
that your count is off by a bead or so, don't
worry. Just finish off the stitch as best you
can, and move on to the next one. No one,
and I mean no one, will ever know.

BOTH VERSIONS

Stretch and condition 2½ yd. (2-3m) of
thread. Thread a needle. String a stop
bead, and center it in the middle of the
thread. Pick up an 8º seed bead, the
ladybug or decorative pewter bead, and
the other 8 º.

To make the Ice Berries colorway, proceed to "First Swag" instructions, and
then continue with "Second Swag" and
"Third Swag" instructions.

To make the Amber Drop colorway, *skip*
the "First Swag" instructions, proceed to
"Second Swag," and then continue with
"Third Swag" instructions.

FIRST SWAG*

1 *For the Ice Berries colorway only.
Pick up 40 color A 11º seed beads, two
color B 11º seed beads, two 15º seed
beads, a 6mm bead, two 15ºs, and a B.
Sew back through the first B and 15 As
(figure 2, a–b–c). Pick up 10 As, two Bs,
two 15ºs, a 6mm, two 15ºs, and a B, sew
back through the first B and the 10 As
you picked up, and continue through 10
As in the trunk **(figure 2, d–e–f)**.

NOTE There are no more illustrations for this swag. Just follow the principles laid out in figures 1 and 2. "First B" refers to the B next to the As you sew back through.

2 Pick up 10 As, two Bs, two 15ºs, a 6mm, two 15ºs, and a B, sew back through the first B, the 10 As you picked up, and continue through the next 10 As in the trunk.

3 Pick up 10 As, two Bs, two 15ºs, a 6mm, two 15ºs, and a B, and sew back through the first B and the 10 As you picked up. Continue through the last five As in the trunk, an 8º seed bead, the pewter bead, and the end 8º. Pick up one A, eight 15ºs, and an A, and sew through the end 8º, the pewter bead, and 8º, and down through 10 As in the trunk.

4 Pick up 13 As, two Bs, two 15ºs, a 6mm, two 15ºs, and a B, and sew back through the first B, 13 As, and down 10 As in the trunk. Repeat. Next, pick up five As, two Bs, two 15ºs, a 6mm, two 15ºs, and a B, and sew back through the first B, five As, and sew down through five As in the trunk.

5 Pick up three As, two Bs, two 15ºs, a 6mm, two 15ºs, and a B, and sew back through the first B and three As. Sew up through three As in the trunk. Pick up four As, two Bs, two 15ºs, a 6mm, two 15ºs, and a B, and sew back through the first B and four As. Sew up through seven As in the trunk and down through seven As in the closest branch with 10 As.

6 Pick up two As, two Bs, two 15ºs, a 6mm, two 15ºs, and a B, and sew back through the first B and two As. Continue up through three As in the branch. Pick up three As, two Bs, two 15ºs, a 6mm, two 15ºs, and a B, and sew back through the first B and three As. Sew up through four As in the branch. Sew up through five As in the trunk. Sew down through 10 As in the closest branch with 13 As in it.

7 Pick up two As, two Bs, two 15ºs, a 6mm, two 15ºs, and a B, and sew back through the first B and two As. Sew up

SUPPLIES

ICE BERRIES

- **1** pewter ladybug bead (TierraCast)

- **58** 6mm top-drilled round frosty blue Czech glass beads

- **2** 8º seed beads (lime-lined AB)

- 11º seed beads

  - **4.5g** color A (light sapphire teal-lined)

  - **2g** color B (pale violet-lined crystal AB)

- **1.25g** 15º seed beads (aqua purple-lined)

- Size D or equivalent beading thread

- Sizes 10, 12, and 13 long beading needles

- Stop beads

- Conditioner

- Thread snips

AMBER DROP COLORS

- **1** 6-8mm pewter spacer bead

- **37** 6x4mm Czech glass teardrops

- **2** 8º seed beads (dark amber)

- 11º seed beads

  - **2g** color A: metallic green

  - **1.5g** color B: ceylon chartreuse

- **.75g** 15º seed beads (peach-lined crystal AB)

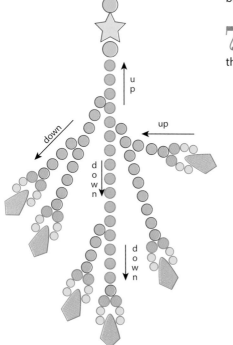

figure 1

8º	seed bead
11º	seed bead, color A
11º	seed bead, color B
15º	seed bead, color C

6mm top-drilled round bead

pewter bead

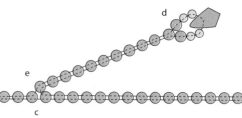

figure 2

through five As in the branch. Pick up four As, two Bs, two 15⁰s, a 6mm, 15⁰s, and a B, and sew back through the first B and four As. Sew up through three As in the branch, pick five As, two Bs, two 15⁰s, a 6mm, two 15⁰s, and a B, and sew back through the first B and five As. Sew up through two As in the branch and five As in the trunk. Sew down through seven As in the nearest branch with 10 As in it.

8 Pick up two As, two Bs, two 15⁰s, a 6mm, two 15⁰s, and a B, and sew back through the first B and two As. Sew up through three As in the branch, pick up four As, two Bs, two 15⁰s, a 6mm, two 15⁰s, and a B, and sew through the first B and four As. Sew up through four As in the branch and fives As in the trunk. Sew down through 10 As in the next branch with 13 As in it.

9 Pick up two As, two Bs, two 15⁰s, a 6mm, two 15⁰s, and a B, and sew back through the first B and two As. Sew up through three As in the branch, pick up four As, two Bs, two 15⁰s, a 6mm, two 15⁰s, and a B, and sew back through the first B and four As. Sew up through five As in the branch, pick up five As, two Bs, two 15⁰s, a 6mm, two 15⁰s, and a B, and sew back through the first B and five As. Sew up through the last two As in the branch and five As in the trunk. Sew down through seven As in the last branch.

10 Pick up two As, two Bs, two 15⁰s, a 6mm, two 15⁰s, and a B, and sew back through the first B and two As. Sew up through four As in the branch, pick up four A, two Bs , two 15⁰s, a 6mm, two 15⁰s, and a B, and sew back through the first B and four As. Sew up through the last three As in the branch. Secure the thread in the main trunk, and end the thread.

SECOND SWAG

1 If this is your first swag (Amber Drop colorway), proceed to step 2. If this is your second swag (Ice Berries colorway), remove the stop bead and thread a needle onto the thread.

2 Pick up 30 As, two Bs, two 15⁰ beads, a 6mm, two 15⁰ beads, and a B. Sew back through the first B and up through five As. Pick up four As, two Bs, two 15⁰s, a 6mm, two 15⁰s, and a B. Sew back through the first B and the four As. Sew up through five As in the trunk. Pick up five As, two Bs, two 15⁰s, a 6mm, two 15⁰s, and a B. Sew back through the first B and five As. Sew through six As in the trunk. Pick up six As, two Bs, two 15⁰s, a 6mm, two 15⁰s, and a B. Sew back through the first B bead and six As. Sew up through seven As in the trunk. Pick up seven As, two Bs, two 15⁰s, a 6mm, two 15⁰s, and a B. Sew back through the first B and seven As. Sew up through the rest of the beads in this trunk.

3 Continue through the 8⁰, the decorative bead, the next 8⁰, the beads in the loop, and back through the 8⁰s and the decorative bead. Continue through three As in this swag.

4 Pick up eight As, two Bs, two 15⁰s, a 6mm, two 15⁰s, and a B. Sew back through the first B and eight As. Sew down through four As in the trunk and four As in the closest branch. Pick up two As, two Bs, two 15⁰s, a 6mm, two 15⁰s, and a B. Sew back through the first B and two As. Sew up three As in the branch, stopping one A away from the trunk.

5 Pick up two As, two Bs, two 15⁰s, a 6mm, two 15⁰s, and a B. Sew back through the first B and two As. Sew up through the last beads in the branch. Sew down three As beads in the trunk.

6 Pick up five As, two Bs, two 15⁰s, a 6mm, two 15⁰s, and a B. Sew back through the first B and five As. Sew down through four As in the trunk. Sew down through two As in the nearest branch. Pick up three As, two Bs, two 15⁰s, a 6mm, two 15⁰s, and a B. Sew back through the first B and three As. Sew up through two As in the branch and down three As in the trunk.

7 Pick up three As, two Bs, two 15⁰s, a 6mm, two 15⁰s, and a B. Sew back through the first B bead and three As. Sew down through three As in the trunk. Sew down three As in the next branch. Pick up an A, two Bs, two 15⁰s, a 6mm, two 15⁰s, and a B. Sew back through the first B bead and the A bead next to it. Sew up through three As in the branch and down two As in the trunk.

8 Pick up four As, two Bs, two 15⁰s, a 6mm, two 15⁰s, and a B. Sew back through the first B and four As. Sew down through three As in the trunk. If your thread is not coming out of the base of the fork of the last two branches keep sewing until your thread is there. Then continue through the first two As beads in the longer branch.

9 Pick up A, two Bs, two 15⁰s, a 6mm, two 15⁰s, and a B. Sew back through the first B and the A. Sew up through

five As in the trunk, skipping a branch, and sew down two As in the second branch. Pick up an A, two Bs, two 15ºs, a 6mm, two 15ºs, and a B. Sew back through the first B and the A. Sew up through two As in the branch. Sew up through five As in the trunk and one A in the branch with three As.

10 Pick up four As, two Bs, two 15ºs, a 6mm, two 15ºs, and a B. Sew back through the first B and four As. Sew up through one A in the branch and up five As in the trunk, skipping another branch. Pick up five As, two Bs, two 15ºs, a 6mm, two 15ºs, and a B. Sew back through the first B and five As. Sew up two As in the trunk and down two As in the next branch. Pick up two As, two Bs, two 15ºs, a 6mm, two 15ºs, and a B. Sew back through the first B and two As. Sew up through two As in the branch. Sew up five As in the trunk, skipping a third branch.

11 Pick up an A, two Bs, two 15ºs, a 6mm, two 15ºs, and a B. Sew back through the first B and the A next to it. Sew up through two As in the trunk and down five As in the last branch. Pick up two As, two Bs, two 15ºs, a 6mm, two 15ºs, and a B. Sew back through the first B and two As. Sew up through three As in the branch. Pick up two As, two Bs, two 15ºs, a 6mm, two 15ºs, and a B. Sew back through the first B and two As. Sew through the remaining beads in the branch. Secure the thread in this swag's trunk.

THIRD SWAG

1 If you are making the Ice Berries colorway, stretch and condition 4 ft. (1.2m) of thread. Thread a needle and string a stop bead. Slide it to 10 in. (2.5cm) from the end of the thread. Sew up through the 8º, the decorative bead, and the other 8º and around the loop. Continue through the 8º and decorative beads. If you are making the Amber Drops colorway, simply remove the stop bead and thread a needle onto the thread.

2 Pick up 23 As, two Bs, two 15ºs, and a B. Sew back through the first B and up three As Pick up two As, two Bs, two 15ºs, a 6mm, two 15ºs, and a B. Sew back

through the first B and two As. Sew up five As in the trunk. Pick up four As, two Bs, two 15ºs, a 6mm, two 15ºs, and a B. Sew back through the first B and four As. Sew up through three As in the trunk.

3 Pick up six As, two Bs, two 15ºs, a 6mm, two 15ºs, and a B. Sew through the first B and four As; this is a short branch. Pick up three As, two Bs, two 15ºs, a 6mm, two 15ºs, and two Bs. Sew back through the first B and three As. Sew up the remaining beads in the branch and sew up three As in the trunk.

4 Pick up seven As, two Bs, two 15ºs, a 6mm, two 15ºs, and a B. Sew back through the first B and three As; this is another short branch. Pick up two As, two Bs, two 15ºs, a 6mm, two 15ºs, and a B. Sew through the first B and two As. Sew up three As in the branch. Pick up four As, two Bs, two 15ºs, a 6mm, two 15ºs, and a B. Sew back through the first B and four As. Sew through the last bead in the branch and up three As in the trunk.

5 Pick up seven As, two Bs, two 15ºs, a 6mm, two 15ºs, and a B. Sew through the first B and three As. Pick up two As, two Bs, two 15ºs, a 6mm, two 15ºs, and a B. Sew through the first B and two As. Sew up three As in the branch.

6 Pick up four As, two Bs, two 15ºs, a 6mm, two 15ºs, and a B. Sew back through the first B and four As. Sew through the last bead in the branch and sew up three As in the trunk. Pick up seven As, two Bs, two 15ºs, a 6mm, two 15ºs, and a B. Sew back through the first

B and three As. Pick up two As, two Bs, two 15ºs, a 6mm, two 15ºs, and a B. Sew back through the first B and two As. Sew up three As in the branch. Pick up four As, two Bs, two 15ºs, a 6mm, two 15ºs and a B. Sew through the first B and four As. Sew through the last A in the branch and up the remaining beads in the trunk.

7 Sew up through the 8ºs, the decorative bead, around the loop and back through the decorative and 8º beads. Pick up an A, two Bs, two 15ºs, a 6mm, two 15ºs, and a B. Sew back through the first B and A. Sew up through the 8ºs, the decorative bead, and the loop again. Bring your needle back through the bottom 8º, so your thread is not too close to the mini swag you just did. Pick up an A, two Bs, two 15ºs, a 6mm, two 15ºs, and a B. Sew through the first B and the A. Sew through the 8ºs, the decorative bead, and the loop again. Secure the thread in this swag's trunk. If you still have a tail, remove the stop bead and secure the tail in any of the trunks.

WREATH

As children, we knew Christmas was coming when wreaths started appearing on doors all around the neighborhood. My mother, who was no Martha Stewart except when it came to knitting, always bought ours at the supermarket. The lady next door (on the other side from the cardinal people) collected pine cones and various evergreen branches and dried leaves, and wired these together with a huge fancy bow to make a new one every year. This little wreath is one that can be enjoyed year after year.

Supplies

GREEN WREATH

- **20** 8º seed beads (silver-lined green AB)
- 11º seed beads
  - **2g** color A (silver-lined green)
  - **.75g** color B (spicy mustard gold)
  - **21** color C (opaque red)
- Bow charm (gold, TierraCast)
- 30mm gold beading hoop
- **4 in. (10cm)** 24-gauge gold craft wire
- Size D or equivalent beading thread
- Size 10 beading needles
- Conditioner
- Thread snips
- Flush cutters

WHITE WREATH COLORS
(shown on pg. 95)
- 8º seed beads: silver-lined crystal AB
- Color A: 11º silver-lined crystal AB
- Color B: 11º silver
- Color C: 11º silver-lined light siam
- Bow charm, beading hoop, craft wire: silver

NOTE The main body of the wreath is a variation on that old classic, the daisy chain stitch. Two wreaths make a fantastic pair of earrings for someone who likes huge, show-stopper earrings. Beading hoops are a fairly common finding — make sure you get the kind with a hole in the metal connector as shown in **figure 1**. Check with your local bead store. If you can't find a hoop with a hole, wrap the bow wires around the neck of the loop. Then wrap the wires around the hoop as shown in the photo.

ORNAMENT

1 Stretch and condition 2 yd. (1.8m) of thread. Pick up nine color A 11º seed beads, and tie a knot so the beads form a ring. Leave a 6-in. (15cm) tail. Sew through two As (be careful and don't pull the knot inside a bead). Pick up an 8º seed bead. Count over four beads, and sew through the fourth and third As, in that order **(figure 2, a–b)**.

2 Pick up seven As, and sew through the fourth and third beads from the previous ring. Pick up an 8º, and sew through the fourth and third beads of the new ring **(figure 3, a–b)**. Repeat this step until you have 20 cells. Be careful not to flip the strip as you go, because if you do, you will not end up with an open circle.

3 Open the hoop and slide the wire through the 8ºs. Make sure your wreath is lying on the front side of the hoop. Close the hoop. Pick up two As, look for the tail, and count down two

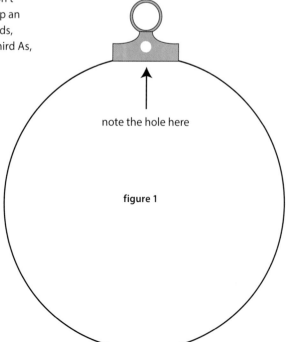

note the hole here

figure 1

○ 8º seed bead

○ 11º seed bead, color A

○ 11º seed bead, color B

○ 11º seed bead, color C

beads. Sew up through these two beads. Pick up three As, and sew through two As in the other end ring as shown **(figure 4, a–b)**. Continue sewing through five As **(c–d)**.

4 Note that there are three beads on the outside of each cell in the wreath. Pick up two As, three color B 11º seed beads, and two As. Sew through the first bead in the group of three beads two cells over and the neighboring bead in the group of three one cell over **(figure 5)**. Bring your thread up in front of the seven-bead swag you just sewed in place. Repeat this step 20 times. Always bring your thread to the front before picking up a new swag. After you finish the 20th swag, bring your thread to the front as usual. Pick up two As, three Bs, and two As, and sew to the back of the first swag (indicated by the gray circles) and sew through the two beads in the groups of three **(figure 6)**. Sew through all the swags again to strengthen them.

5 Scatter the color C 11º seed beads around the wreath in groups of one, two, or three beads as suggested in **figure 7**. Do not place any beads in the top three cells — you need this space for the bow. End the threads.

6 Center the bow bead on the wire, and bend the wires to the back of the bow. Run the wires through the lower little hole in the hoop — it is more or less centered in the cell that does not have an 8º. Wrap the wires around the hoop on the back side to hold the bow in place **(photo)**. Trim the excess wire. Use the remaining little loop on the hoop for an ornament hanger or an earring wire, if you decide to make earrings.

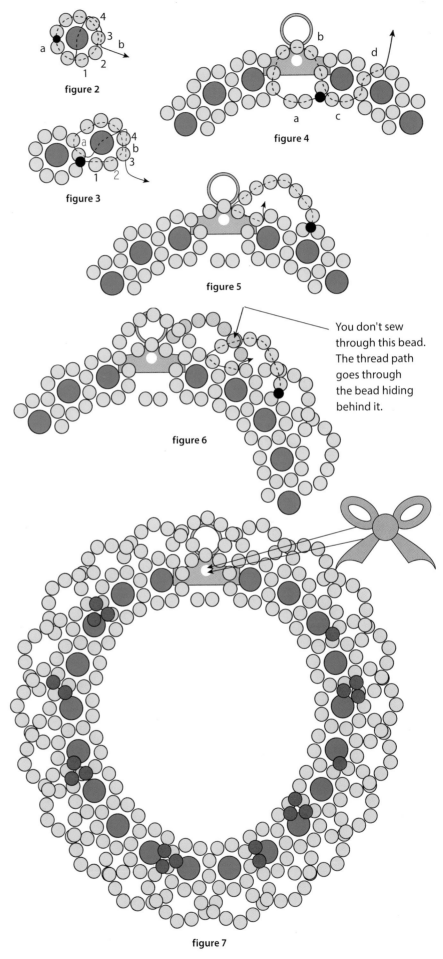

figure 2

figure 3

figure 4

figure 5

You don't sew through this bead. The thread path goes through the bead hiding behind it.

figure 6

figure 7

CHAPTER 3
Intermediate Ornaments

RUM-PAH-PUM DRUM

A comedienne once pointed out that no new mother would appreciate some kid banging on a drum just after she's given birth. Even so, the little drummer boy has become a Christmas icon—perhaps because in each of us there is a toddler who would love to bang a drum.

Supplies

- 11º seed beads
  - **2.5g** color A (light beige)
  - **.5g** color B (gold)
- 11º cylinder beads
  - **1.5g** color C (silver-lined light bronze)
  - **.75g** color D (silver-lined cobalt)
  - **1.75g** color E (silver-lined dyed raspberry)
- **.5g** 15º seed beads, color F (gold)
- Size D or equivalent beading thread
- Sizes 10 and 12 beading needles
- Conditioner
- Thread snips

DRUM HEAD

NOTE This part of the drum is made with flat, circular peyote stitch. You can set up the beads for each round before picking any up. This helps keep track of where you are in the pattern. When you run out of beads, it is time to step up. If you do this, make sure you count the repetitions for each round carefully. The references to colored outlines indicate which beads you will be picking up for that step.

1 Stretch and condition 1 yd. (.9m) of thread. Pick up three color A 11º seed beads, and slide them to 6 in. (15cm) from the end of the thread. Tie a knot so the beads form a tight circle. Sew through an A **(figure 1, pink outlines)**. Pick up an A, sew through the next A. Repeat twice, and step up through the first A **(blue outlines)**.

2 Pick up three As, and sew through the next A. Repeat twice, and step up through the first A **(figure 2, red outlines)**. Pick up an A, and sew through the next A. Repeat eight times, and step up through the first A **(green outlines)**.

Pick up two As, and sew through the next A. Pick up an A, and sew through the next A. Pick up an A, and sew through the next A. Repeat the section between the asterisks twice. Step up through the first A **(pink outlines)**.

3 *Pick up an A, and sew through the next A; pick up an A, and sew through the next A; pick up two As, and sew through an A; pick up an A, and sew through an A.* Repeat the section between the asterisks twice. Step up through an A **(figure 3, pink outlines)**. **Pick up two As, and sew through an A. Pick up an A, and sew through two As. Pick up an A, and sew through an A. Pick up two As, and sew through an A.** Repeat the section between the double asterisks twice. Step up through an A. ***Pick up an A, and sew through an A. Pick up an A, and sew through an A. Pick up three As, and sew through an A. Pick up an A, and sew through an A. Pick up an A, and sew through an A. Pick up an A, and sew through an A.*** Repeat the section between the triple asterisks twice. Step up through an A.

4 *Pick up a color B 11º seed bead, and sew through an A. Pick up a B, and sew through three As. Pick up a B and sew through an A. Repeat this last stitch three times. * Repeat the section between asterisks twice. Step up through a B. **Pick up a color C 11º cylinder bead, sew through a B, pick up a C, and sew through the middle A in the next group of three As. Pick up a C, and sew through a B. Repeat this last stitch four times.** Repeat the section between the double asterisks twice. Step up through a C.

5 Work two rows of regular peyote stitch using only Cs. Remember to step up after each row. End the threads in the As (do not secure it in the Bs or Cs).

6 Repeat steps 1–5 to make a second drum head.

DRUM BODY

1 Stretch and condition 1½ yd. (1.4m) of thread. Secure your thread, and make sure your needle and thread are coming out of the bead indicated in the **pattern**. It is important that you start in the right

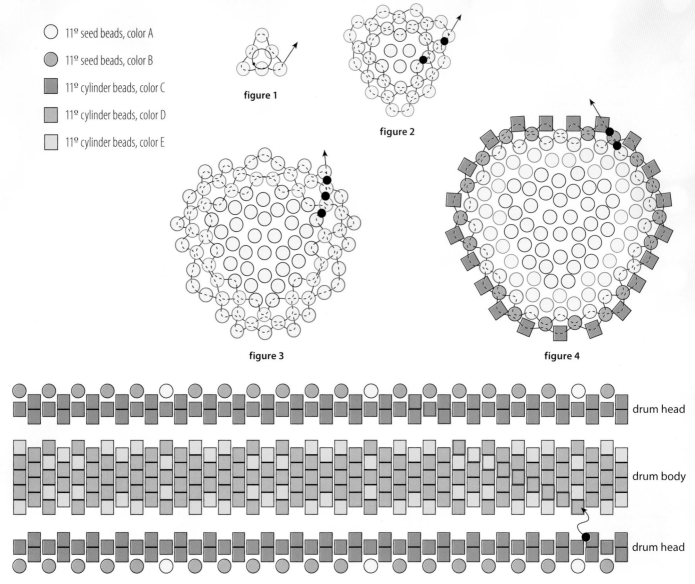

Legend:
- ○ 11º seed beads, color A
- ● 11º seed beads, color B
- ■ 11º cylinder beads, color C
- ■ 11º cylinder beads, color D
- ■ 11º cylinder beads, color E

figure 1

figure 2

figure 3

figure 4

drum head

drum body

drum head

pattern (read from the bottom up)

place because if you don't the drum body design will not line up properly with the heads. You can follow the pattern or follow the row-by-row instructions below. The beads outlined in red are the starting beads of each round.

2 Round 1: Work in peyote stitch to complete this pattern three times: color D 11º cylinder bead, color E 11º cylinder bead, E, D, D, and two Es. Step up through a D.
Round 2: Stitch this pattern three times: D, E, D, E, D, E, D. Step up through a D.
Round 3: Stitch this pattern three times: D, D, E, E, D, D, E. Step up through a D.
Rounds 4–6: Stitch three rounds using only D beads. Step up through a D.

Round 7: Stitch this pattern three times: E, E, D, D, E, D, D. Step up through an E.
Round 8: Stitch this pattern three times: E, D, E, D, D, E, D. Step up through an E.
Round 9: Stitch this pattern three times: D, E, E, D, E, E, D. Step up through a D.

3 Arrange up the drum heads so the three As in the outermost rows line up. Zip the body to the remaining drum head. Once the drum is zipped together, sew through beads until you have sewn through one of the As you used to line up the heads. Pick up 12 15º seed beads, and sew through the aligned A on the other drum head. Sew back through these beads again to tighten the snare. Sew to the next alignment A, and repeat.

Repeat again with the third set of alignment beads.

4 Make the loop: After you've finished the third snare made with the 15º s, continue sewing through beads until you have sewn through the fourth B on the edge. Pick up eight 15º s. Sew through the third B, an A, and the fourth B again. Sew through all these beads again to strengthen and tighten the loop. End the threads. Tie a ¼-in. (6mm) ribbon through the loop to make a strap for the drum.

Supplies

- 11º cylinder beads
  - **4.75g** color A (opaque white ceylon)
  - **2g** color B (opaque red)
  - **1.75g** color C (silver)
- 11º seed beads
  - **2g** color D (silver)
- Size D or equivalent beading thread
- Sizes 10 and 12 beading needles
- Stop bead
- Conditioner
- Thread snips

ABSTRACT BOW

Sometimes a decoration doesn't have to be anything in particular. Diagonal peyote lets this decoration be whatever you see. It's a bit like a bow, a bit like what a frost fairy would wear if it was also a court jester, and a bit like a star.

NOTE Refer to increasing and decreasing with diagonal peyote, p. 10. What makes diagonal peyote have diagonal edges rather than straight edges is the way you decrease on one side and increase on the other. There is a definite rhythm to it once you get going. Keep track of where you are with the pattern. When you increase, one of the beads you pick up is the first bead for a row that doesn't exist yet — and that can make it difficult to anticipate which color bead you are supposed to pick up.

BOW

1 Stretch and condition 2 yd (1.8m) of thread. Thread a needle onto one end. Pick up a stop bead, and center it on the thread. Pick up a color A 11º cylinder bead, a color B 11º cylinder bead, two As, a color C 11º cylinder bead, two As, a B, two As, a C, two As, a B, two As, a C, two As, a B, a color D 11º seed bead, and a B **(figure 1, a–b)**. You are working from the inside of the 'V' to the point. Sew back through the last A **(b–c)**.

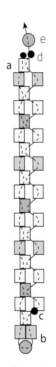

- ☐ 11º cylinder bead, color A
- ▧ 11º cylinder bead, color B
- ▨ 11º cylinder bead, color C
- ◯ 11º seed bead

figure 1

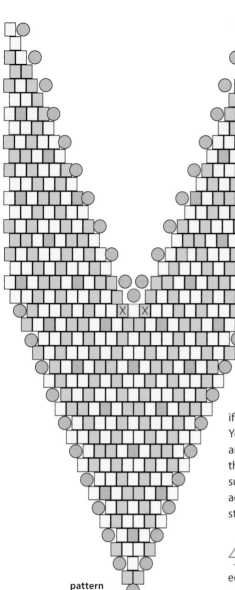

pattern

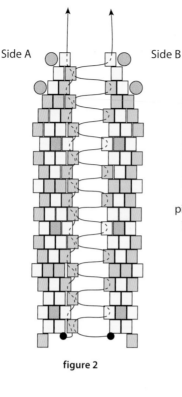

Side A   Side B

figure 2

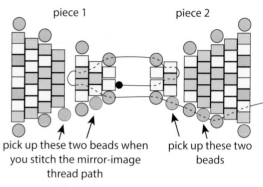

piece 1   piece 2

pick up these two beads when you stitch the mirror-image thread path

pick up these two beads

figure 3

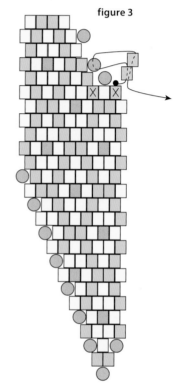

figure 4

2 Work peyote stitch with these beads in the order given: A, A, B, A, A, B, A, A, B **(c–d)**. After you have added the last B, pick up a D **(d–e)**. Sew through all the beads again except for the D at the top — stop when you sew through the topmost A.

3 Begin working in peyote stitch: Start with either of the Bs marked with an "X" on the **pattern**. Follow the pattern as you work from the center through the upwards slant on one side only. You will decrease and turn around on the outside edge. When you reach that point on the chart, refer to p. 9 if necessary. You will always pick up a D and then a cylinder to turn around along the outside edge. After you complete your turn-around, resume peyote stitching. When you reach the inside of the "V," you will increase and turn around. Refer to p. 9

if necessary when you reach this point. You will always pick up a cylinder, a D, and another cylinder. Sew back through the first cylinder you picked up. Make sure the turn-around beads are snug against the beadwork. Begin peyote stitching for the next row.

4 Continue working in peyote stitch while decreasing on the outside edge and increasing on the inside edge. Finish out the row after you have stitched the 10th increase in place. Leave the thread for now — you may find it helpful to string a stop bead and slide it up against the beadwork.

5 Remove the stop bead from the other end of the thread, and thread a needle. Repeat step 3–4 until you have 10 decreases and 10 increases. After you've completed the 10th increase and row, stitch a row of Bs until you sew through the A at the end **(figure 2, side A)**. Do not trim the excess thread. Remove the stop bead from the remaining thread, and thread a needle. Zip the two sides together **(side B)**. Secure only this thread in the diamond shapes.

6 Repeat steps 1–5 to make a second piece. Arrange them horizontally so the top points face each other and you can see the red diamonds that are centered on top. Make sure the threads

are exiting two As that are opposite each other. If they are not, sew one thread so that it is exiting the right A. Otherwise, thread a needle onto one of the two threads. Starting at the black dot, follow the thread path shown in **figure 3** to connect the two pieces. First, with the thread from piece 1, sew through the A, B, A, and D in piece 2. Next, sew through the D, A, B, B, and A in piece 1. Now sew through the D in piece 2. Pick up a D (red outline) and sew through the next D. Pick up a D (red outline) and sew through the following D. Secure the thread in the white diamond As next to the red diamond Bs. Follow the same thread path with the other needle to stitch a mirror image on the other piece.

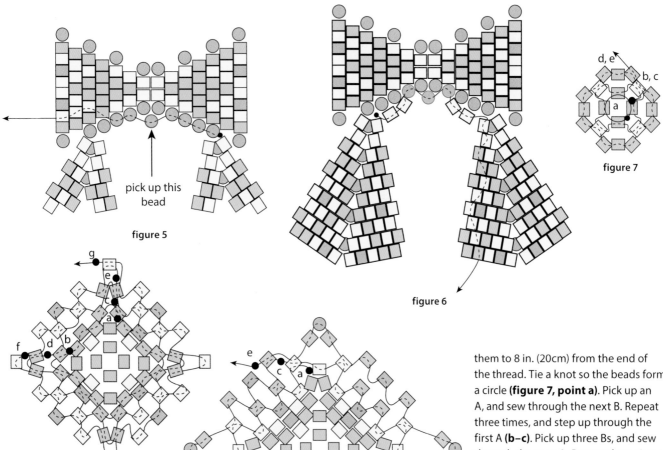

pick up this bead

figure 5

figure 6

figure 7

figure 8

figure 9

them to 8 in. (20cm) from the end of the thread. Tie a knot so the beads form a circle **(figure 7, point a)**. Pick up an A, and sew through the next B. Repeat three times, and step up through the first A **(b–c)**. Pick up three Bs, and sew through the next A. Repeat three times, and step up through the first B **(d–e)**.

11 Pick up two Bs, skip a B and sew through the next B, pick up a C, and sew through the next B **(figure 8, a–b)**. Repeat three times, and then sew through a B **(c)**. *Pick up two Bs, and sew through the next B. Pick up an A, and sew through the next C. Pick up an A and sew through the next B **(c–d)**.* Repeat the section between the asterisks three times. Sew through the first B **(e)**. **Pick up an A, and sew through the next B. Pick up an A, and sew through the next A. Pick up a C, and sew through the next A. Pick up an A, and sew through the next B **(e–f)**.** Repeat the section between the double asterisks three times. Step up through a point A **(g)**.

12 Pick up an A, and sew through the next A. Pick up a B, and sew through the next C. Pick up a B, and sew through the next A. Pick up an A, and sew through the next A. **(figure 9, a–b)**. Repeat these stitches three times, and step up through the first A **(c)**. *Pick up a B, and sew through the next B. Pick up a C, and sew through the next B. Pick up a

7 Repeat steps 1–4 to make the first half of a third piece. Remove the stop bead, and stitch until you are ready to do the first increase. Instead of picking up a D, you will sew through the D on the finished half **(figure 4)**. Continue peyote stitching, sewing through a D every time you increase rather than picking one up. Stop when you have 10 decreases and 10 increases — do not stitch that extra row of Bs. After you have stitched the last row of beads, sew back up and through the last A. Do not trim your thread. Make a second piece like this one.

8 Hold one of the pieces you just made so that you are looking down into it — the Ds from the increases will be barely visible if you can see them at all. With one of the outer threads, follow the thread path shown in **figure 5** to attach this piece to the previously connected pieces. Pick up the D indicated by the gray circle with a red outline. Secure

the thread in the second row of white diamonds. Follow the thread path with the other outside thread — this time you will sew through the center D rather than pick one up.

9 With the remaining needles, exiting one of the new pieces, pick up two As, and sew through three Ds (indicated by pink outlines in **figure 6**). Pick up two As, and sew through the cylinder on the corresponding piece with a thread coming out of it. Secure the thread along the edge. Follow the thread path with the remaining needle and thread — but don't pick up any beads this time.

10 Stretch and condition 1 yd. (.9m) of thread. Pick up four Bs, and slide

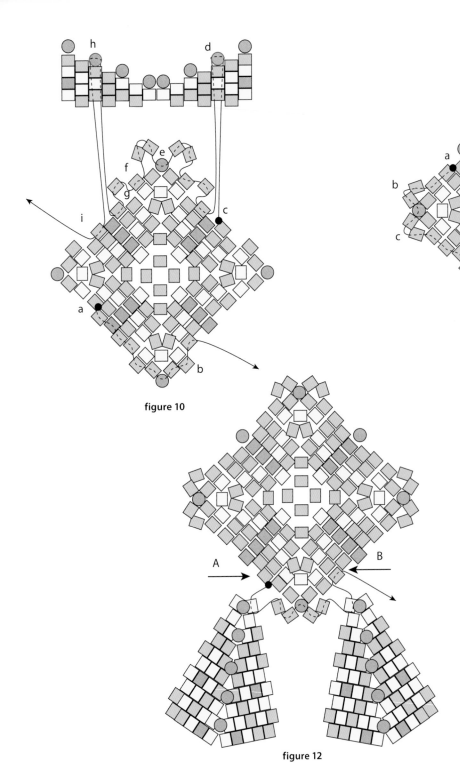

figure 10

figure 11

A   B

figure 12

next B. Sew through the other bead indicated by the pink outline. Sew through the next B in the knot **(d–i)**.

15 Pick up a B, and sew through the next B. Pick up two Bs, and sew through the next D. Pick up two Bs, and sew through the next B. Pick up a B, and sew through the next B. Pick up a C, and sew through the next B **(figure 12, a–b)**. Repeat these stitches once. Repeat it again, but this time, sew through a D instead of picking up a bead **(point e)**. Continue sewing through beads until you sew through the D at the top **(point f)**. Pick up 10 Ds. Sew back through the first one. Sew through the D at the top again and through the other 10 Ds again. You can sew through them all again if you want to make the loop extra strong. Continue sewing along the edge of the square until you reach the bead indicated by arrow A in **figure 12**. Hold the beadwork so it is facing you — you will see the Ds that zipped the inner "V"s together. Sew through an A in the main beadwork, two Bs in the square, a D in the square, two Bs in the square, another D in the main beadwork, and then through the B indicated by arrow B. I recommend circling around the square again so that you can sew the connecting As again for more strength. End the threads.

B, and sew through the next A. Pick up a B, a D, and a B, and sew through the next A **(c–d)*** Repeat the section between the asterisks three times. Step up through the first B **(e)**.

13 Pick up a B, and sew through the next C. Pick up a B, and sew through the next B. Pick up a B, and sew through the next B, a D, and a B. Pick up a B, and sew through the next B **(figure 10, a–b)**. Repeat these stitches three times, and step up through the first B.

14 It's time to sew this square "knot" to the main bow. Sew through the D indicated by the pink outline **(c–d)**. Sew through the next B on the knot, pick up a B, and sew through the next B. Pick up two Bs, and sew through the next D. Pick up two Bs, and sew through the next B. Pick up a B and sew through the

Supplies

WHITE AND PURPLE STAR

- **30** 6mm two-hole triangle beads (CzechMates white)

- **2** 4–6mm fire-polished beads (matte light amethyst)

- **60** 2mm fire-polished beads (purple suede)

- **1.75g** 11º seed beads (lilac ceylon)

- **1** 20-gauge 2-in. (5cm) headpin

- Toho One-G or K-O thread

- Sizes 10 and 12 beading needles

- Stop beads

- Conditioner

- Thread snips

- Roundnose pliers

- Chainnose pliers

- Flush cutters

PURPLE AND GREEN STAR COLORS

- Two-hole triangle beads: transparent dusty cedar or amethyst

- 4–6mm fire-polished beads: polychrome pink olive

- 2mm fire-polished beads: saturated metallic kale

- 11º seed beads: galvanized silver

RED AND GOLD STAR COLORS

- Two-hole triangle beads: siam ruby

- 4–6mm fire-polished beads: garnet

- 2mm fire-polished beads: matte flax

- 11º seed beads: dyed rose silver-lined alabaster

GEODESIC BALL

Geodesic figures are essential to learn if you want to do three-dimensional beadwork. How fortunate that they make great ornaments! You may find that they are a bit like potato chips: It's hard to make just one.

NOTE Refer to making wrapped loops, p. 11. Be sure to snug the beads in each stitch up to the previous stitch's beads before making the next stitch.

ORNAMENT

1 Arrange the two-hole triangle beads as shown in **figure 1**. Always pick up the triangle by the hole designated in the instructions. Stretch and condition 5 ft. (1.52m) of thread. String a stop bead, and slide it to 6 in. (15cm) from the end of the thread. Pick up two 11º seed beads, a triangle by the left hole, and two 11º s. Sew through the right hole and the first two 11º s (**figure 2, a–c**). Pick up three 11º s, a triangle by the left hole, and two 11º s, and sew through the right hole and the last two 11º s (**d–f**). Repeat this stitch three times. Pick up an 11º, and

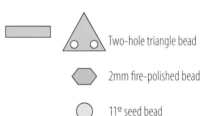

Two-hole triangle bead

2mm fire-polished bead

11º seed bead

left hole   right hole

figure 1

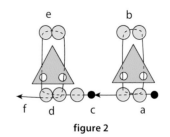

figure 2

45

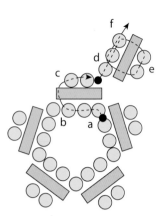

figure 3

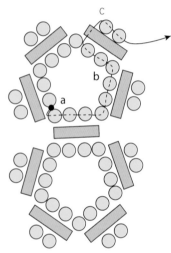

figure 4

sew through the first two 11ºs, triangle, and two 11ºs (**figure 3, a–c**).

2 Pick up three 11ºs, a triangle by the left hole, and two 11ºs, and sew through the right hole and the adjacent two 11ºs (**d–f**). Repeat three times. Pick up an 11º. Sew through eight 11ºs, the adjacent triangle, and the next two 11ºs (**figure 4, a–b–c**).

3 Repeat step 2 twice. You will now have four pentagons. Pick up three 11ºs, a triangle by the left hole, and two 11ºs, and sew through the right hole and two 11ºs. Pick up an 11º, and sew through the two 11ºs at the other end of the strip, as indicated in **figure 5, a–b.** This will connect the ends together. Pick up three 11ºs, a triangle by the left hole, and two 11ºs, and sew through the right hole and the last two 11ºs. Repeat this stitch once (**c**). Pick up an 11º, and sew through the two 11ºs indicated in **d**. Continue through nine more 11ºs, a triangle, and two 11ºs, ending at **e**.

4 From now on, you will see the beadwork take on three dimensions. Pick up an 11º, and sew through two 11ºs in the adjacent unit. Then pick up three 11ºs, a triangle by the left hole, and two 11ºs, and sew through the right hole and the last two 11ºs. Repeat this stitch twice (**figure 6, a–b–c–d**). Pick up an 11º and sew through the first two 11ºs your thread exited at the start of this step (**e**). Continue through six more 11ºs, the adjacent triangle, and the next two 11ºs, ending at **f**.

5 Pick up an 11º, and sew through two 11ºs twice (**g–h**). Then pick up three 11ºs, a triangle by the left hole, and two 11ºs, and sew through the right hole and two 11ºs. Repeat this stitch once (**i–j**). Pick up an 11º, and sew through 11 11ºs, a triangle, and two 11ºs (**k–l**).

6 Repeat step 5 twice.

7 Pick up an 11º, and sew through two 11ºs three times (**figure 7, a–b**). Pick up three 11ºs, a triangle by the left hole, and two 11ºs, and sew through the right hole and the first two 11ºs. Pick up an 11º, and sew through two 11ºs (**c–d**). Sew through twelve 11ºs, a triangle, and two 11ºs. Pick up an 11º, and sew through two 11ºs five times. Set this needle aside for a moment. Remove the stop bead, and thread a needle onto the tail. Sew through three 11ºs, a triangle, and two 11ºs. Pick up an 11º, and sew through two 11ºs. Repeat this stitch four times to cinch up the ring of 11ºs on this side. Remove the needle, but do not trim the tail thread.

8 Using the working thread again, sew through a triangle. Pick up a 2mm fire-polished bead, and sew through a triangle. Repeat this stitch twice (**figure 8, a–b–c**). Sewing through 11ºs, triangles, and 2mms when necessary, work your way around the dodecahedron (that's what this shape is called because it has 12 sides), sewing a 2mm into every corner. End the thread and the tail after you have sewn in all 60 2mms.

9 String a 4–6mm fire-polished bead onto a headpin. Feed the end of the headpin through one of the gaps where the triangles meet. String the other 4–6mm on the headpin. Make sure the two beads hold the dodecahedron snugly, and make a wrapped loop.

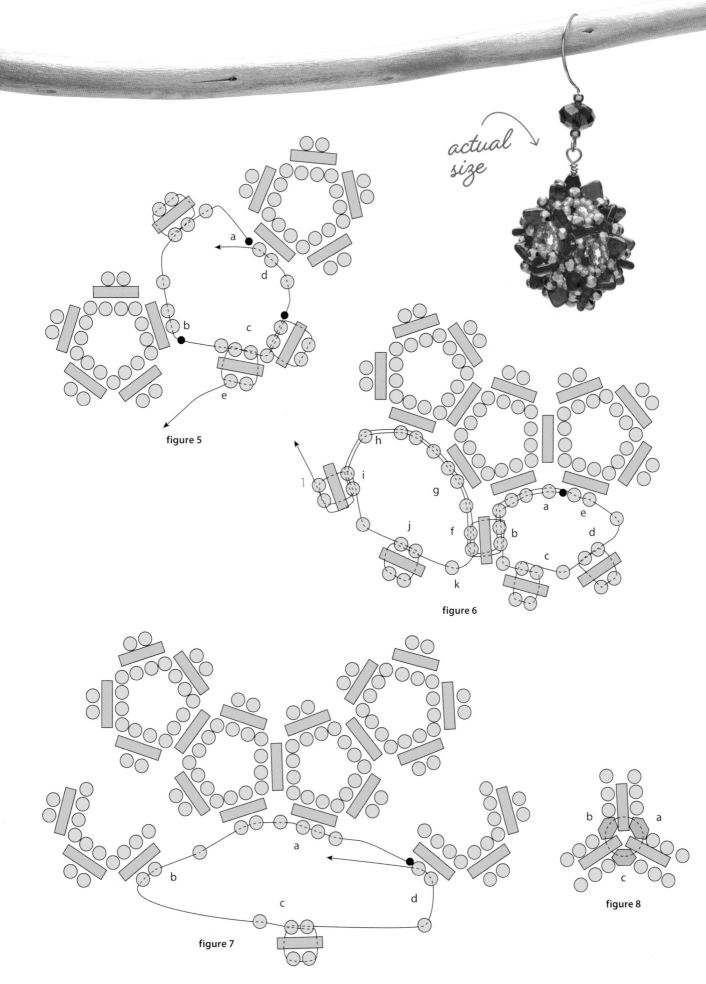

actual size

figure 5

figure 6

figure 7

figure 8

"PAPER" LANTERNS

Colorful paper lanterns make everything look ready for a party. Really, they couldn't look more fun if they tried. Sadly, they don't last forever but this beaded version is likely to last a very long time. A grouping of them would look adorable hanging in a small area.

NOTE See techniques for making a tassel on page 12. Also, review the section "Adding and ending thread — bead weaving" on p. 10. Review the section on making a wrapped loop in basics on p. 11, if needed.

LANTERN

1 Stretch and condition 2 yd. (1.8m) of thread. Pick up five color A 11º seed beads, and slide them to 6 in. (15cm) from the end of the thread. Tie a knot, and sew through one bead. Do not pull the knot into the bead **(figure 1, a)**. Pick up an A, and sew through the next A. Repeat this stitch four times, and step up through the first A added **(b–c–d–e–f–g)**.

2 Pick up a color B 11º seed bead and an A, and sew through the next A. Repeat five times. Sew through the first B **(figure 2, red outlines)**. Pick up an A, sew through the next A, pick up an A, and sew through the next B. Repeat these stitches four times. Continue through the first A **(green outlines)**.

Supplies

RED LANTERN
- 11º seed beads
  - **4g** color A (salmon-lined crystal)
  - **4g** color B (yellow-lined crystal)
  - **4.5g** color C (opaque red luster)
- **1** 6mm fire-polished beads (crystal)
- **2** 3mm spacers (silver)
- **2** 12mm bead caps (silver)
- **2** 20 gauge 2-in. (5cm) headpins (silver)
- Tassel (see p. 12 to make your own)
- Size D thread or an equivalent of your choice
- Size 11 beading needles
- Conditioner
- Thread snips
- Roundnose pliers
- Chainnose pliers
- Flush cutters

BLUE LANTERN COLORS
- 11º seed beads
  - Color A: matte white
  - Color B: opaque light blue
  - Color C: blue iris
- 6mm fire-polished bead: crystal

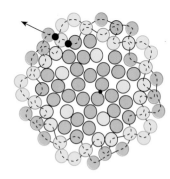

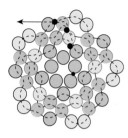

figure 1   **figure 2**   **figure 3**

- 🔵 11º seed bead, color A
- ⚪ 11º seed bead, color B
- 🔘 11º seed bead, color C

Pick up an A, sew through the next A, pick up two Bs, and sew through the next A. Repeat these stitches four times. Step up through the first A **(outer ring with black outlines)**.

3 Pick up a B, sew through the next B, pick up an A, sew through the next B, pick up a B, and sew through the next A. Repeat this sequence four times. Continue through the first B **(figure 3, red outlines)**. Pick up an A, sew through an A, pick up an A, sew through a B, pick up two Bs, and sew through a B. Repeat this sequence four times. Continue through the first A **(green outlines)**.

4 Now that you have the idea of how doing increases in peyote stitch works, the next illustrations will only show a couple of the sequences and how they fit into the previous round. Read **figure 4** from the bottom up and right to left. The bead sequence is in parentheses at the beginning of each row.

Round 1: A, B, C, B, (Pick up an A, sew through an A, pick up a B, and sew through a B. Pick up a C, sew through a B, pick up a B, and sew through an A. Repeat the sequence four times, and step up through the first A.)

Round 2: B, C, C, B (Pick up a B, sew through a B, pick up a C, and sew through a C. Pick up a C, sew through a B, pick up a B, and sew through an A. Repeat the sequence four times, and step up through the first B.)

Round 3: C, A, C, two Bs (Pick up a C, sew through a C, pick up an A, sew through a C, pick up a C, and sew through a B. Pick up two Bs, and sew through a B. Repeat the sequence four times, and step up through the first C.)

Round 4: A, A, C, B, C (Pick up an A, sew through an A, pick up an A, and sew through a C. Pick up a C, sew through a B, pick up a B, and sew through a B. Pick up a C, and sew through a C. Repeat the sequence four times, and step up through the first A.)

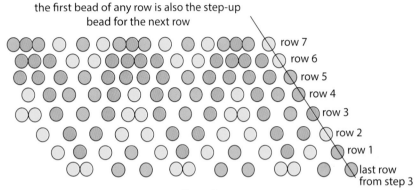

the first bead of any row is also the step-up bead for the next row

row 7
row 6
row 5
row 4
row 3
row 2
row 1
last row from step 3

figure 4

Round 5: A, C, C, C, C (Pick up an A, sew through an A, pick up a C, and sew through a C. Pick up a C, sew through a B, pick up a C, and sew through a C. Pick up a C, and sew through an A. Repeat the sequence four times, and step up through the first A.)

Round 6: B, C, two Cs, C, B (Pick up a B, sew through a C, pick up a C, and sew through a C. Pick up two Cs, sew through a C, pick up a C, and sew through a C. Pick up a B, and sew through an A. Repeat the sequence four times, and step up through the first B.)

Round 7: B, A, C, A, B, A (Pick up a B. Sew through a C. Pick up an A. Sew through a C. Pick up a C. Sew through a C. Pick up an A. Sew through a C. Pick up a B. Sew through a B. Pick up an A. Sew through a B. Repeat the sequence four times and step up through the first B.)

5 Now that you're proficient, if not an expert at handling these increases, the rest of the rounds are abbreviated below. Repeat each sequence five times. Many people find it helpful to lay out each row before they stitch it in place. I lay mine out from right to left because I'm right-handed.

Round 8: C, C, C, C, A, A.

Round 9: A, 2B, A, B, A, B.
Round 10: B, A, B, C, B, B, C.
Round 11: A, A, B, C, A, C, B.
Round 12: 2B, A, B, A, A, B, A.
Round 13: C, B, A, C, A, C, A, B.
Round 14: C, B, A, C, C, A, B, C.
Round 15: B, C, A, C, A, C, B, A.
Round 16: C, C, A, A, C, C, C, C.
FIRST HALF ONLY: secure thread back in the bowl of the first half — do not make any knots in the last couple of rounds. Secure the tail and trim all excess threads.

6 Make a second bowl just like the first one. Do not secure your working thread after step 5. Instead, stitch the zip row: B, B, A, B, B, A, A, A, repeating the sequence five times, and stepping up through the first B. Leave the working thread alone, but end the tail.

7 String a fire-polished bead on a headpin. Slide the headpin through the center of one bowl. Stack a bead cap and a 3mm spacer onto the headpin, and make a wrapped loop. Repeat with the other bowl, sliding the tassel into the loop before wrapping. Line up the big color A vees, and zip the two halves together. End the thread.

ZIG-ZAG-ZIG BALL

There is always a place for a classic ball ornament. Diagonal lines are wonderfully bold when made with herringbone stitch. The increases give this ornament a textured look at the top and bottom which provides an interesting counterpoint to the smoothness around the center.

NOTE Read the sections on wrapped loops (p. 11) and tassel-making on p. 12. There are two secrets to this ornament: one, have a soft touch with your tension; two, choose three colors of seed beads that are comparable in size. Sometimes 11ºs run a little on the thin side, and sometimes a little on the chunky side. While you can make the pattern work with bead colors that are obviously different in size, it does make it trickier to manage your tension.

INTRODUCTION TO HERRINGBONE STITCH

This stitch is made up of columns and rows. Think of each column as having two beads and a row as being made up of beads in different columns that are level with each other **(figure 1)**. You pick up two beads for every stitch, and sew down through one bead and up through another to complete the stitch **(a–b)**. This stitch has a stepping-up feature, similar to the one in peyote stitch. To step up in herringbone, you pick up two beads, sew down through one bead and up through two **(c–d–e)**.

For a while, you will sew in a sort of cross between peyote and herringbone. Once the ball has reached its full diameter, you will start stitching only herringbone. Pull down on the thread to tighten your tension but remember to keep your touch soft. Look at how the beads are angled — you want your beads to do the same thing. If they don't, your tension is probably too tight.

ORNAMENT

1 Stretch and condition a comfortable length of thread, and thread a needle. Pick up two color A 11º seed beads, two color B 11º seed beads, and two color C 11º seed beads. Sew through the beads again, and continue through an A. Pick

up two As, and sew down through an A and up through a B. Pick up two Bs, and sew down through a B and up through a C. Pick up two Cs, and sew down through a C and up through two As **(figure 2, a–c)**. Pick up two As, and sew through an A. Pick up two Cs, and sew up through one B. Pick up two Bs, and sew down through a B. Pick up two As, and sew up through a C. Pick up two Cs, and sew through a C. Pick up two Bs, and sew up through two As **(d–j)**.

2 Work a row of herringbone around the circle, picking up whatever color you just sewed through. Step up through two As **(figure 3, black dotted lines)**. Pick up two As, and sew through an A **(pink dotted lines, a)**. Pick up a B, and sew through a C **(b)**. Pick up two Cs, and sew through a C **(c)**. Pick up an A, and sew through a B **(d)**. Pick up two Bs, and sew through a B **(e)**. Pick up a C, and sew through an A **(f)**. Pick up two As, and sew through an A **(g)**. Pick up a B, and sew through a C **(h)**. Pick up two Cs, and sew through a C **(i)**. Pick up an A, and

sew through a B **(j)**. Pick up two Bs, and sew through a B **(k)**. Pick up a C, and sew through 2As **(l)**.

3 It is especially important that you have soft tension in this row. Sew through an A **(figure 4, a)**. Pick up a B, and sew through a B. Pick up a B, and sew up through one C and down through the next C **(b, c)**. Pick up an A, and sew through an A. Pick up an A, and sew up through a B and down through the next B **(d, e)**. Pick up a C, and sew through a C. Pick up a C, and sew up through one A and down through the next A **(f, g)**. Pick up a B, and sew through a B. Pick up a B, and sew up through a C and down through the next C **(h, i)**. Pick up an A, and sew through an A. Pick up an A, and sew up through a B and down through the next B **(j, k)**. Pick up a C, and sew through a C. Pick up a C and sew through one A **(l-m)**. Work a row of herringbone stitches around the circle. Always pick up two of whichever color you just sewed through. Step up through two As at the end.

Supplies

PASTEL BALL
- 11º seed beads

  - **4.5g** color A (semi-matte silver-lined purple)

  - **4.5g** color B (semi-matte silver-lined pink)

  - **4.5g** color C (semi-matte silver-lined mint green)

- **2** 6mm fire-polished beads (clear)
- **2** 12mm bead caps (silver)
- **2** 3mm spacer beads (silver)
- **2** 20-gauge 2-in. (5cm) headpins (silver)
- Tassel (see p. 12 to make your own)
- Size D thread or equivalent
- Sizes 10 and 12 beading needles
- Conditioner
- Thread snips
- Roundnose pliers
- Chainnose pliers
- Flush cutters

ROYAL BALL COLORS
- 11º seed beads

  - Color A: matte metallic blue

  - Color B: matte white

  - Color C: gold

11º seed bead, color A

11º seed bead, color B

11º seed bead, color C

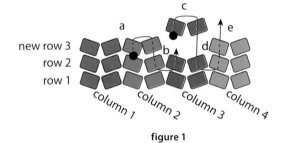

new row 3
row 2
row 1

column 1 column 2 column 3 column 4

figure 1

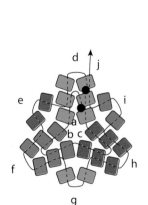

figure 2

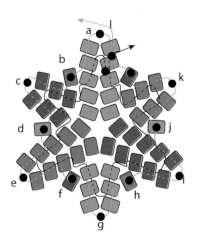

figure 3

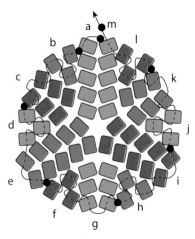

figure 4

4 Make sure your long columns have six pairs of beads and the short columns have four pairs. The columns are separated by groups of five beads. Sew through an A **(figure 5, a)**. Pick up a C, and sew through two Bs. Pick up an A, and sew through two Cs. Pick up a B, and sew through two As. Pick up a C, and sew through two Bs. Pick up an A, and sew through two Cs. Pick up a B, and sew through two As. Pick up a C, and sew through two Bs. Pick up an A, and sew through two Cs. Pick up a B, and sew up through one A **(b–m)**.

5 You're now going to do a modified herringbone stitch all around the edge. You'll sew through the lone bead between columns as well as sewing down through a bead in one column and up through a bead in the next. Pick up two As and sew through an A, a C, and a B **(figure 6, a, b)**. Pick up two Bs, sew through a B, an A, and a C **(b, c)**. Pick up two Cs, and sew through a C, a B, and an A **(c, d)**. Pick up two As and sew through an A, a C, and a B **(d, e)**. Pick up two Bs and sew through a B, an A and a C **(e, f)**. Pick up two Cs and sew through a C, a B and an A **(f, g)**. Pick up two As and sew through an A, a C, and a B **(g, h)**.

Pick up two Bs and sew through a B, an A, and a C **(h, i)**. Pick up two Cs and sew through a C, a B, and an A **(i, j)**. Pick up two As and sew through an A, a C, and a B **(j, k)**. Pick up two Bs and sew through a B, an A, and a C **(k, l)**. Pick up two Cs and sew through a C, a B, and two As **(l, m)**.

6 This next row is very similar. You will still add to the herringbone columns with the color bead that is already established, but Instead of sewing through a bead between columns, you will pick up a bead the same color as the bead already in place between rows **(figure 7)**. You will end this step by stepping up through two As **(a)**.

7 This row is also very similar. This time, as you add herringbone stitches to the columns you will float two beads between columns. These floater beads are the same color as the single beads already in place. Keep your tension soft in this row — you will need to be able to manipulate the floater beads so that you can use them for herringbone stitches. Step up through two As **(figure 8)**.

8 As you can see, the column heights are uneven. Fix this by sewing around the edge with this stitch pattern: Sew down through two beads in a

column. Sew up through a floater bead. Pick up two beads the same color as the floater beads. Sew down through a floater bead. Sew up through two beads in the next column **(figure 9, a, b)**. Repeat all around the edge. End by sewing through two As after you have added beads above the last floater beads **(c)**.

9 Stitch three rows of herringbone stitches. Maintain the colors established in each column. Begin tightening your tension with these rows. It will still be a while before you see the sides start to draw up into a bowl shape. You will always step up through the longest A column.

10 Refer to the zig-zag chart before going any further **(figure 10)**. There are five diagonal rows, and you will be working them from the bottom up.
Row 1: Pick up a B and an A; sew through an A and a C. Pick up an A and a C; sew through a C and a B. Pick up a C and a B; sew through a B and an A. Repeat this sequence a total of eight times. Step up through an A and a B.
Row 2: Pick up two Bs; sew through two As. Pick up two As, sew through two Cs, Pick up two Cs; sew through two Bs.

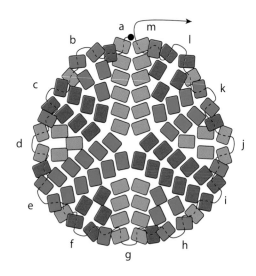

Note that this illustration picks up after completing the row of herringbone stitches at the end of step 3.

figure 5

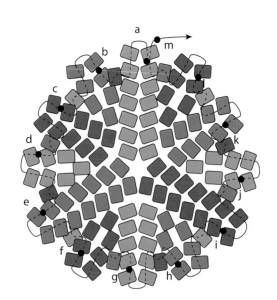

figure 6

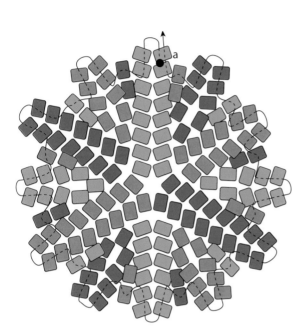

figure 7

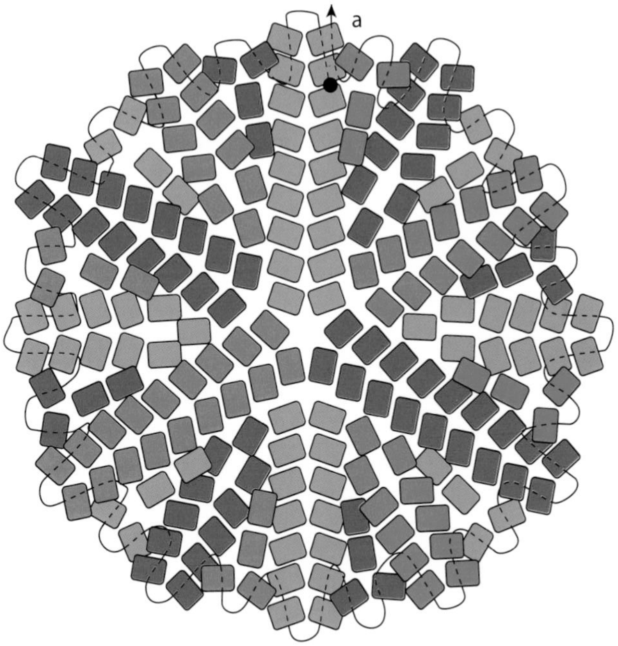

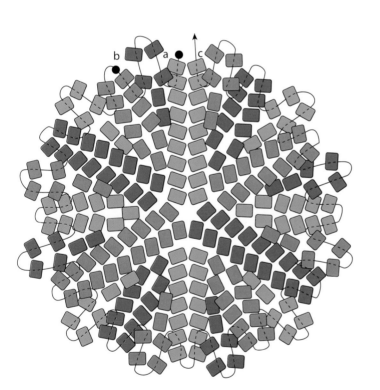

figure 8

figure 9

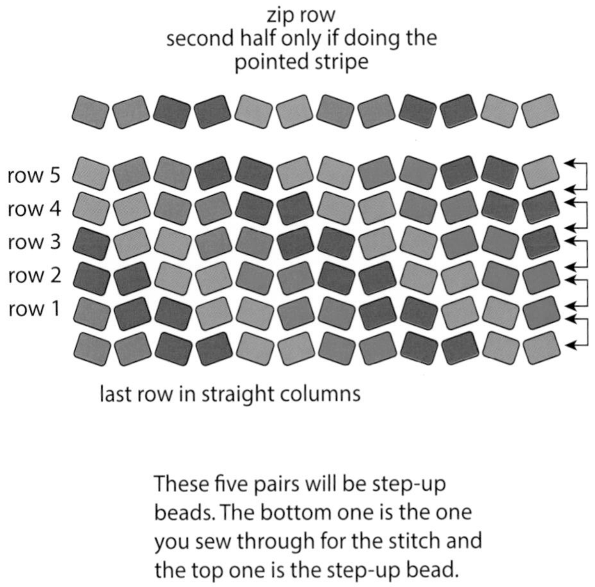

zip row
second half only if doing the
pointed stripe

row 5
row 4
row 3
row 2
row 1

last row in straight columns

These five pairs will be step-up
beads. The bottom one is the one
you sew through for the stitch and
the top one is the step-up bead.

figure 10

Repeat this series a total of eight times. Step up through two Bs.

Row 3: Pick up a C and a B; sew through a B and an A. Pick up a B and an A; sew through an A and a C. Pick up an A and a C; sew through a C and a B. Repeat this series eight times. Step up through two Bs.

Row 4: Pick up two Cs; sew through two Bs. Pick up two Bs; sew through two As. Pick up two As; sew through two Cs. Repeat this series eight times. Step up through two Cs.

Row 5: Pick up an A and a C; sew through a C and a B. Pick up a C and a B; sew through a B and an A. Pick up a B and an A; sew through an A and a C. Repeat this sequence eight times. Step up through a C and an A. Sew through just the beads in this last row again.

11 Repeat steps 1–10 to make a second half. If you want your stripes to look like the ones in the blue, white, and gold example, do everything exactly the same. If you want your stripes to look like the pastel example, turn the beadwork inside out before starting the three rows of straight herringbone stitches. This means that you will not be stitching in your usual direction so it will be a little uncomfortable at first. If you will need a zip row, do not stitch through the last row of beads again.

Zip row: only stitch this row if you want a pointed stripe as shown in the pastel example. Stitch the zip row after you have finished the five diagonal rows **(figure 10)**. Sew through just the beads in the zip row again. Do not connect the halves yet.

12 String a fire-polished bead on a headpin. Pass the headpin through the center hole of the bowl. The bead goes inside the bowl. String a bead cap and a spacer bead, and make a wrapped loop, sliding the tassel into the loop before completing the wraps. Use the remaining headpin, fire-polished bead, bead cap, and spacer to make a wrapped loop on the other half.

13 Line up the two halves and zip them together. If you want the pastel stripes arrange the lines to form a point **(figure 11)**. If you want the other style stripe choose a color and line up those color stripes. The other two colors will be offset **(figure 12)**.

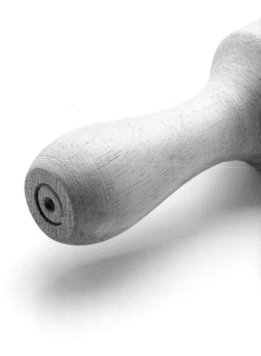

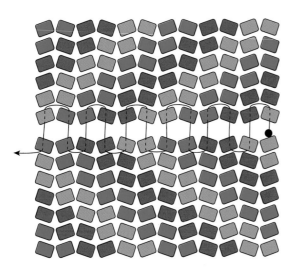

figure 11

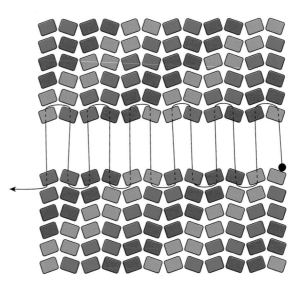

figure 12

SUGAR COOKIE STARS

Nothing says "It's holiday time!" quite the way iced cut-out cookies do. One year, my grandmother showed us grandchildren how to make ornaments with homemade clay-dough dyed with food coloring and painted to look like iced cookies. They were fragile and didn't last for more than a couple of years, but the memory is forever. These beaded cookie stars are for you, Grandma.

NOTE Review flat peyote stitch and diagonal peyote on p. 9.

STARS

1 Stretch and condition 1 yd. (.9m) of thread. String a stop bead and center it on the thread. Pick up 10 color A 11º cylinder beads, three color B 11º cylinder beads, an A, and a 15º seed bead. Sew back through the last A and B (**figure 1, a–b**). Pick up a B, skip the next B, and

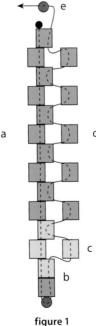

figure 1

sew through the following B **(c)**. Pick up an A, skip an A, and sew through the next A, five times **(d)**. Pick up a C **(e)**.

2 Sew through all the cylinders and the 15º at the bottom again, following

Supplies

GREEN COOKIE

- 11º cylinder beads
  - **6g** color A (matte opaque light mint)
  - **2.75g** color B (matte transparent emerald green)
- **1g** 15º seed beads (galvanized silver)
- Toho One-G, K-O or C-Lon AA thread
- Size 10 and 12 beading needles
- Stop bead
- Conditioner
- Thread snips

the same thread path. When you get back to the top, do not sew through the 15º next to the tail again.

3 Begin working in peyote stitch by picking up either A indicated with an "X" in **figure 2**. Follow the chart, and refer to the sections on decreasing and increasing in diagonal peyote, p. 10. Note that there are four increases and five decreases. Stitch a final row of As after the last decrease turn-around, and stop after sewing through the last A in the previous row. Leave your thread — you will need it later.

4 Remove the stop bead. Stitch the other half of this piece as a mirror image of the first half. Leave the thread for this half as well — you will also need this thread later. Make nine pieces.

5 Stretch and condition 1 yd. (.9m) of thread, and repeat step 1. Pick up a 15º, and sew along one side of the strip until you sew through the 15º at the bottom **(figure 3, a)**. Pick up eight 15ºs, and sew through the 15º at the tip of the strip again. Sew through the loop a couple of times to strengthen it, and then sew up the other side of the strip. Do not sew through the 15º at the end with the tail. Repeat steps 3–4 to finish this last (tenth) point. Leave the needle on the thread after you finish step 4.

6 Pick up a B, and sew through an A on another point that has a thread exiting it **(figure 4, a)**. It helps to pull on it while you are sewing into the bead. Pick up an A, and sew through the A where you started **(b)**. Sew through the B and the A again. Continue up the side a few beads before securing the thread **(c)**. Do

not sew through the As and 15ºs along the increase edge. Trim the excess from this thread only.

7 Thread a needle onto the tail in the "V". Sew through the adjacent B and an A. Pick up a 15º, and sew through the A between the points **(figure 5, a)**. Pick up a 15º, and sew through an A, B, A, and B **(b)**. Sew up a few edge As before ending this thread **(c)**. Sew together two strips of five points in this way.

8 Intertwine the two strips as shown in **photo a**. Be careful not to tangle the four remaining threads. Follow steps 6–7 to connect the sides indicated in **photo b**. Pass one of the remaining ends over and the other end under as shown in **photo c**. Follow steps 6–7 to sew these ends together.

9 Stretch and condition 1 yd. (.9m) of thread. String a stop bead, and slide it to 8 in. (20cm) from the end of the thread. Find the point with the loop, and hold the star so that you can see six complete color B diamonds. The seventh

will be masked by the point overlapping the front of the loop point. Sew through two Bs indicated in **figure 6, a**. Sew through the 15º **(b)**. Continue sewing through 15ºs and As along the edge until you sew through the last A **(c)**.

10 This point you have sewn through will overlap the next point. Sew up through the corresponding A on the next point **(d)**. Sew through the As at points c and d again. Make sure the A at point c is on top of the A at point d. Continue sewing up the side through 15ºs and As until you sew through the fifth 15º **(e, f)**. Sew through the two Bs indicated in **g, h**. Sew through the 15º indicated in **i**. Connect all 10 points. When you return to the tip of the loop point, sew to meet the tail. Don't tie the threads together, but do end them.

figure 3

■ 11º cylinder bead, color A

□ 11º cylinder bead, color B

● 15º seed bead

figure 2

A

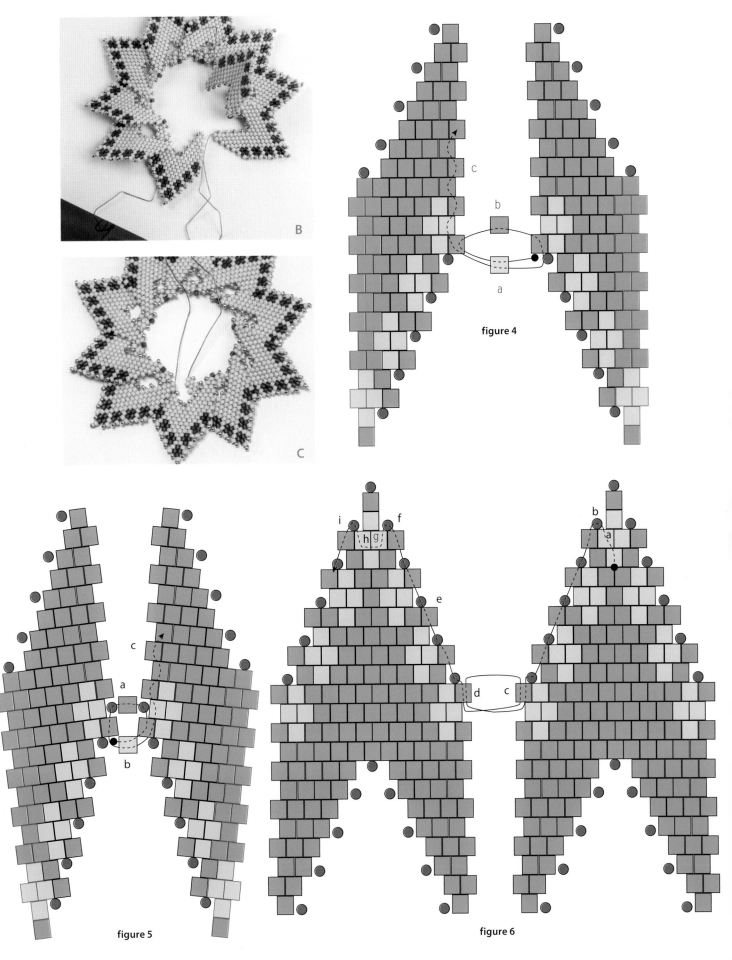

figure 4

figure 5

figure 6

CHAPTER 4

Constructed Ornaments

BELL SWAG

From little tiny jingly baubles to massive church versions, all bells are magical because the sound of them can evoke so many different moods and memories. These little Christmas bells would make a lovely gift to a couple in honor of their first holiday together—especially if you make the bells in their wedding colors.

Supplies

- 11º seed beads
  - **6.25g** color A (silver-lined crystal AB)
  - **2.5g** color B (silver-lined blue-green)
  - **2.5g** color C (black-lined transparent red)
  - **1.25g** color D (gold)
- **5** 4mm fire-polished beads (clear)
- **5** 8mm bead caps (gold)
- **5** 3mm spacers (gold)
- **5** 2-in. (5cm) 20-gauge headpins (gold)
- 18 in. (46cm) flat Ultrasuede cord (or chain)
- Size D thread or equivalent
- Sizes 10 and 12 beading needles
- Thread snips
- Beeswax
- Awl (to pierce Ultrasuede)

NOTE Review the section on making wrapped loops, p. 11, if necessary.

1 Stretch and condition 1 yd. (.9m) of thread. Pick up five color A 11º seed beads. Slide them to 8 in. (20cm) from the end, and tie the thread in a knot so the beads form a circle. Sew through an A, but do not pull the knot inside the bead. Pick up an A, and sew through an A five times. Continue through the first A **(figure 1, red outlines)**.

2 Pick up an A, a color B 11º seed bead, and an A, and sew through an A. Repeat this stitch five times. Continue through an A and a B. Pick up an A, a color C 11º seed bead, and an A, and sew through the next B. Repeat this stitch five times. Continue through an A and a C **(outer black outlines)**.

3 Pick up an A, a B, and an A, and sew through the next C. Repeat five times, and continue through an A and a B.

4 Pick up an A, a C, and an A. Sew through the next B. Repeat five times. Continue through an A and a C.

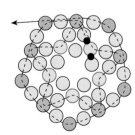

figure 1

5 Repeat step 3. Sew through just the As in this round again, skipping the Bs. Step up through the first B. Pick up two As, a C , and two As, and sew through a B **(figure 2, a)**. Repeat this stitch five times. Sew through these beads again, skipping the Cs. Step up through the first C. Pick up five As, and sew through the next C **(b)**. Repeat this stitch five times. Continue through five As.

6 Pick up a color D 11° seed bead, and sew through the next five As **(figure 3, a)**. Repeat five times. Continue through the first D. Pick up two As, a D, and two As, and sew through the next D **(b)**. Repeat this stitch five times. Continue through two As, a D, and two As. Pick up a B, and sew through two As, a D, and two As **(c)**. Repeat this stitch five times. Continue through a B.

7 Pick up a B, a C, two Ds, a C, and a B. Sew through a B at the point where the bell begins to flare out. It will have one A leading into it and out of it at the top and two As leading in and out at the bottom. Sew back through the last B you picked up **(figure 4, a–b)**. Pick up a C, two Ds, a C, and a B. Sew through the next B on the bell's rim and sew back through the B you just picked up **(c)**. Continue around the rim: First, pick up a C, two Ds, a C, and a B, and then sew through a B in the bell, either at the

rim or where the flare begins. Finally, sew through the B you picked up. Keep doing this until you have one swag left to fill in. For this swag, you only pick up a C two Ds, and a C. Sew through two Bs, one in a swag and the other in the bell rim. End the threads.

8 String a 4mm fire-polished bead on a headpin. Feed the headpin from the inside of the bell to the outside through the hole made by the ring of five As at the top of the bell. String a bead cap and a spacer onto the headpin. Start the loop, but do not complete the wraps yet.

9 Repeat steps 1–8 to make four more bells.

10 Fold over about 4 in. (10cm) of the Ultrasuede, and tie a knot, making a loop big enough to use as a hanger. Trim the short end so that only about ¼ in. (6mm) remains. Poke a hole in the long end just below where the short tail ends. Feed the headpin through the hole, and wrap the loop in place. Poke another hole in the Ultrasuede that is even with the spot where the bell flare starts. Insert another headpin, and wrap a bell in place. Measure, poke holes, and wrap two more bells in place. Make the hole for the fifth bell. Trim the Ultra-suede to ¼ in. (6mm) below the hole. Insert the last bell, and wrap in place.

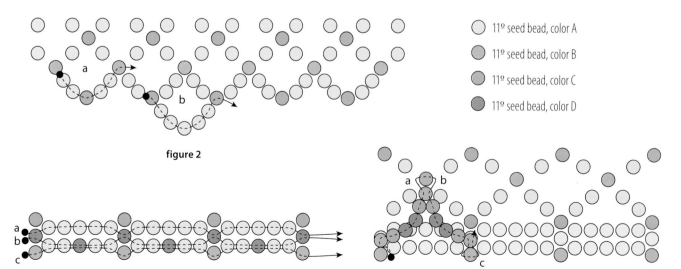

figure 2

figure 3

figure 4

○ 11° seed bead, color A

○ 11° seed bead, color B

○ 11° seed bead, color C

○ 11° seed bead, color D

POINSETTIA FLOWER

There are Christmas cacti and there are Christmas roses, but the poinsettia is the queen of the holiday flowers. You know winter is coming when floral departments start bursting with poinsettias. That brilliant red is actually part of the foliage — the flowers sit inconspicuously in the center of that riot of color.

NOTE This ornament is tied on rather than hung with a hook. Tie it to a branch, a candlestick, or even your dog's harness. A pair of single leaves made with this variation of St. Petersburg stitch make a great pair of earrings. And created, instead, with an assortment of reds, oranges, and yellows, the poinsettia can become harvest foliage to decorate your family's Thanksgiving table.

GREEN LEAVES

1 Stretch and condition 4 ft. (1.22m) of thread. Center a stop bead. Pick up an 11º Demi bead, an 8º seed bead, a Demi, a color A 11º seed bead, four color B 11º seed beads, and an A. Slide them to meet the stop bead, and sew through the middle two Bs so the last four beads form a square **(figure 1)**.

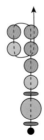

figure 1

Supplies

BOTH COLORWAYS

- **5g** 8º seed beads (lined green AB)
- **3g** 11º Demi seed beads (higher-metallic june bug)
- **18 in. (46cm)** of ¼-in. (6mm) ribbon
- Size D thread
- Sizes 10 and 12 beading needles
- Conditioner
- Size 22 tapestry needle

GREEN LEAVES FOR BOTH COLORWAYS

- 11º seed beads
    - **.75g** color A (semi-matte silver-lined leaf green)
    - **3g** color B (silver-lined rainbow green emerald)
    - **.75g** color G (silver-lined dark peridot)

RED POINSETTIA ONLY

- 11º seed beads
    - **1.75g** color A (semi-matte silver-lined leaf green)
    - **7.5g** color B (opaque red)
    - **.75g** color D (opaque yellow)
    - **12** color E (sour apple luster)
- **1.75g** 15º seed beads, color G (opaque red)

PINK POINSETTIA ONLY

- 11º seed beads
    - **1.75g** color A (semi-matte silver-lined pink)
    - **7.5g** color B (white-lined crystal AB)
    - **.75g** color D (semi-matte daffodil-lined crystal)
    - **12** color E (sour apple luster)
- **1.75g** 15º seed beads, color G (silver-lined light pink)

2 Pick up two Bs and three color G 15º seed beads. Sew back through five Bs and an A **(figure 2)**. Pick up an 8º and a Demi. Sew through the A and B on the left **(figure 3)**.

3 Pick up three Bs and an A. Sew through the middle two Bs again **(figure 4)**.

4 Repeat steps 2–3, following the figures, until you have eight fronds. End by picking up two Bs and three Gs, and sewing back through five Bs, an A, a Demi, and an 8º **(figure 5, a–b)**. Sew through the Demis and 8ºs until you sew through the last 8º. Do not sew through the last Demi **(c)**.

5 Remove the stop bead, and thread a needle onto the long end of the thread. Pick up an A, four Bs, and an A, and sew back through the middle two Bs **(d–e)**. Make seven complete fronds and the bottom of the eighth **(figure 6, a)**.

6 Pick up two Bs, and sew through a B and an A in the ninth frond **(b)**. Continue through the two Bs you just picked up.

7 Pick up two Bs and three Gs **(c)**, and sew back through five Bs and an A. Continue up through an 8º, Demi, A, and five Bs in the ninth (or center) frond. Sew through the Gs, and sew back down through all the beads in the ninth or center frond **(d, e, f)**. Sew through the Demis and 8ºs in the second side of the leaf until you meet the first thread. Tie the threads together. Pull the knot into the bottom 8º. End the threads. Make three green leaves.

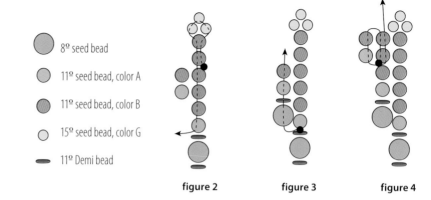

- ○ 8º seed bead
- ○ 11º seed bead, color A
- ◍ 11º seed bead, color B
- ○ 15º seed bead, color G
- ▬ 11º Demi bead

figure 2   figure 3   figure 4

RED AND PINK LEAVES

The same 8ºs and Demis are used in all three color leaves. To make the red leaves: use the same color A as in the green leaves; use 11º opaque red for color B; use 15º opaque red for color G. To make the pink leaves: use 11º semi-matte silver-lined pink for color A; use 11º white lined crystal AB for color B; use 15º silver-lined light pink for color G.

1 Make three red or pink leaves following steps 1–7. Make six more leaves following the **chart**. Refer to steps 6–7 to connect the last frond on side 2 to the center frond.

2 Connect the leaves: Stretch and condition 1 yd. (.9m) of thread. String a stop bead, and slide it to 10 in. (25cm) from the end. Sew through an A, a Demi, an 8º, a Demi, and an A in one green leaf. Sew through these same beads on a second green leaf, and a third **(figure 7)**. Continue through the first A, Demi, 8º, and Demi **(a)**.

3 Sew through a Demi, an 8º, and a Demi in one of the three biggest red leaves. Sew through a Demi, an 8º and a Demi of a green leaf. Sew through a Demi, an 8º, and a Demi of the next green leaf. Sew through a Demi, an 8º, and a Demi of the last big red leaf. Sew through a Demi, an 8º, and a Demi of the third green leaf. Continue through a Demi of the first big red leaf .

4 **NOTE** These 11ºs are all As even though they are different colors. Keep following a circle as you continue to sew the leaves together. Pick up the largest leaf remaining, and sew through

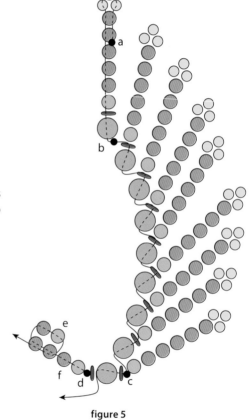

figure 5

an 11º, a Demi, an 8º, a Demi, and an 11º. Sew through an 8º on a red leaf already sewn in place. Continue sewing the remaining leaves in place in this way. Pick them up in order of size, from largest to smallest. Sew through an 11º, a Demi, an 8º, a Demi, and an 11º on the leaf you pick up and only through an 8º of one already sewn into place. End the threads.

Number of leaves	Side 1	center	Side 2
1	7 fronds	1 frond	6 fronds
1	6 fronds	1 frond	5 fronds
1	5 fronds	1 frond	4 fronds
1	4 fronds	1 frond	3 fronds
2	3 fronds	1 frond	2 fronds

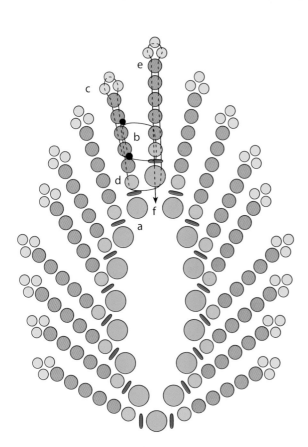

figure 6

color option

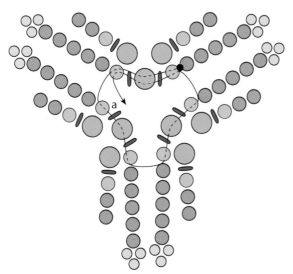

figure 7

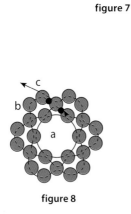

figure 8

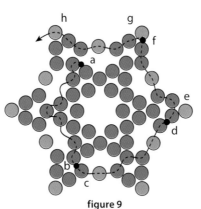

figure 9

FLOWER

5 Stretch and condition 1 yd. (.9m) of thread. Pick up six color D 11º seed beads. Sew through all of them again, leaving an 8-in. (20cm) tail. Sew once more through the first one. Pick up a D, and sew through the next D. Do this six times, and continue through the first D you picked up **(figure 8, a)**. Pick up two Ds, and sew through the next D. Do this six times, and continue through the first D **(b, c)**.

6 Pick up a D, and sew through two Ds. Do this six times, and continue through the first two Ds **(figure 9, a–b)**. Pick up a D, a color E 11º seed bead, and a D, and sew through the next middle D. Do this six times and continue through the first D, E, and D **(c–d)**. Pick up two Ds, and sew through the next D, E, and D. Do this six times, and continue through the first D **(e–f)**. Pick up an E, and sew through two Ds, an E, and two Ds. Do this six times **(g–h)**. End the threads.

FINISH

Thread the ribbon through the tapestry needle. Sew up from the bottom through the center of the flower, and pick up a 6º seed bead. Sew back through the flower and the poinsettia. Center the 6º on the ribbon. String a 6º onto each end of the ribbon. Tie a knot a couple of inches up to keep the beads on the ribbon. Trim the ribbon ends at an angle.

BUGLE

It's unclear why bugles became a Christmas ornament. I'm sure it's not because the little drummer boy needed someone to march with him. I've heard that bugles can symbolize peace, so perhaps that is part of the reason. Of course, maybe it's just because they are shiny, and shiny things always look good on a tree.

NOTE You may want to use Duracoat or PermaFinish gold beads so your bugle remains golden over the years.

BUGLE BASE

1 Work in right-angle weave (RAW) to make the base: Stretch and condition 2 yd. (1.8m) of thread. String a stop bead and slide it to 12 in. (30cm) from the end of the thread. Work four stitches in flat right-angle weave: Pick up four 11º seed beads. Slide them to the stop bead, and sew through the first two beads again so they make a little circle (**figure 1, a**). Pick up three 11º seed beads, and sew through the bead in the completed circle and the first two 11ºs you just picked

up (**b**). Repeat the previous stitch twice (**c–d**). Pick up an 11º, and sew through the end bead in the first ring. Pick up another 11º, and sew through the end bead of the fourth circle. Continue through three beads (**e–g**).

2 Trim the points off the toothpick. Slide the ring of beads onto the toothpick.

3 Pick up three 11ºs, and sew back through the one where you started and the first one you picked up (**figure 2**). Pick up two 11ºs, and sew through the next 11º in the previous row and the 11º in the previous stitch that your

Supplies

- 4 6x4mm oval crystals (clear)
- 4 3mm fire-polished beads (antique gold)
- 6 8º beads (gold)
- 5g 11º seed beads (gold)
- .75g 15º seed beads (gold)
- 1 yd. (.9m) size 4 pearl knotting string or standard micro-macrame cord (red)
- 2 ft. (61cm) ¼-in. (6mm) ribbon (green)
- Size D thread or an equivalent
- Sizes 10 and 12 beading needles
- Stop bead
- Conditioner
- Thread snips
- Round toothpick
- Floral pin or long quilter's pin
- Awl
- Flush cutters

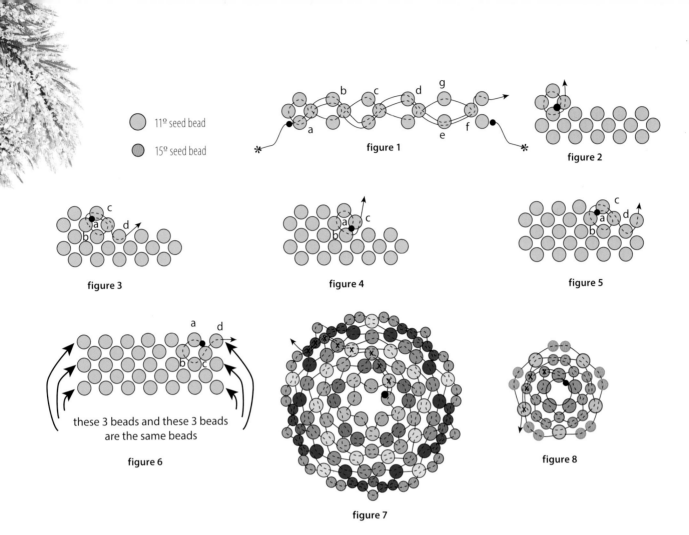

Legend

○ 11º seed bead
◉ 15º seed bead

figure 1

figure 2

figure 3

figure 4

figure 5

these 3 beads and these 3 beads
are the same beads

figure 6

figure 7

figure 8

thread is exiting. Continue through the two you picked up and the next bead in the previous row **(figure 3)**. Pick up two 11ºs, and sew through the edge bead in the previous stitch, the bead your thread exited at the start of this step, and the first bead just picked up **(figure 4)**. Pick up two 11ºs, and sew through the next bead in the previous round and the last bead in the previous stitch. Sew back through the two beads just picked up, the next bead in the previous row, and the first bead in this row **(figure 5)**. Pick up an 11º, and sew through the three beads that complete this square and the top bead of the next square. **(figure 6)**.

4 Repeat step 3 until you have covered the toothpick. If your beadwork is 2 in. (5cm) long and you haven't covered the toothpick, trim the toothpick to fit.

BUGLE ENDS

1 To make the bell, refer to **figure 7**. Each row is identified by a different color circle, and the step-up beads are marked with an "x". Pick up an 11º **(blue**

circles), and sew through an end 11º **(gray circles)**. Do this five times, and step up through the first 11º you picked up. Pick up two 11ºs **(purple circles)** and sew through an 11º **(blue circles)**. Do this five times and step up through the first bead of one of the pairs you picked up. Pick up an 11º **(pink circles)**, and sew through an 11º **(purple circles)**. Do this 10 times and step up through an 11º. Stitch a second round of 10 beads, picking up an 11º **(yellow circles)** and sewing through an 11º **(pink circles)**.

2 Keep referring to **figure 7**. Pick up two 11ºs **(green circles)**, and sew through an 11º **(yellow circle)**. Pick up an 11º **(green circle)**, and sew through an 11º **(yellow circle)**. Do this five times, and step up through only one 11º in the first pair you picked up. Pick up a 15º **(orange circle)**, and sew through an 11º **(green circle)**. Pick up an 11º **(dark orange circle)**, and sew through an 11º **(green circle)**. Do this five times, and step up through a 15º **(orange circle)**. Pick up two 15ºs **(dark blue circles)**.

Sew through an 11º **(dark orange circle)**. Pick up an 11º **(lavender circles)**, and sew through an 11º **(dark orange circle)**. Pick up two 15ºs **(dark blue circles)**, and sew through a 15º **(orange circle)**. Do this five times, and step up through two 15ºs **(dark blue circles)**. Pick up two 15ºs **(pink circles)**, and sew through an 11º **(lavender circles)**. Pick up two 15ºs **(pink circles)**, and sew through two 15ºs **(dark blue circles)**. Pick up a 15º **(pink circle)**, and sew through two 15ºs **(dark blue circles)**. Do this five times, and end the thread.

3 To make the mouthpiece, refer to **figure 8**. The rows are indicated by different colors and the step-up beads are marked with an "x". Thread a needle onto the tail. Sew through the five 11ºs at the end of the tube. Make sure the toothpick is inside these beads. Sew through the first one again. Pick up a 15º, and sew through an 11º. Repeat five times and step up through a 15º **(black outlines)**. Pick up two 15ºs and sew through a 15º. Repeat five times, and

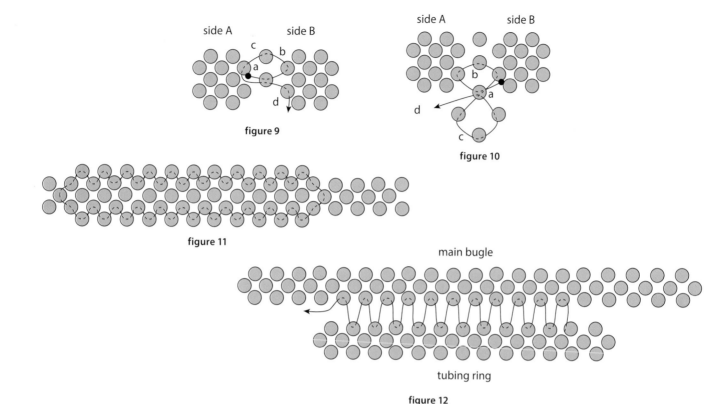

figure 9

figure 10

figure 11

main bugle

tubing ring

figure 12

step up through two 15⁰s (**green outlines**). Pick up an 11⁰, and sew through two 15⁰s. Repeat five times, and step up through an 11⁰ (**red outlines**). Pick up two 15⁰s, and sew through an 11⁰ (**gray outlines**). Repeat five times. End the threads.

4 Bugle tube slide: This is exactly like the RAW bugle base, except that this has a base of three instead of five. Stretch and condition 2 yd. (1.8m) of thread. Pick up four 11⁰s, and sew through the first two 11⁰s again. Pick up three 11⁰s, and sew through the bead where you started plus the first two you picked up. Pick up an 11⁰, and sew through the end bead near the tail. Pick up an 11⁰, and sew through the other end bead to close this ring. Sew through the end bead near the tail again and the next bead. Refer to figures to continue working in RAW. Use the floral or quilter's pin as a stitching form until the beadwork is long enough to hold comfortably. Stitch until the beadwork is 3 in. (7.6cm) long.
Connect the tube: Make sure the tube is not twisted before sewing the ends together. Pick up an 11⁰, and sew through

an end bead on the other side, side B (**figure 9, a–b**). Pick up an 11⁰, and sew through the bead where you started on side A, the first 11⁰ you picked up, and the next end bead on side B (**c–d**). Pick up an 11⁰, and sew through the opposite end bead on side A, the bead connecting the sides, the 11⁰ where you started, and the 11⁰ you just picked up (**figure 10, a–b**). You will see three beads that have not been sewn together yet. Without adding any beads, sew through them and back through the bead you picked up (**c–d**).

5 Attach the tubes: Make sure the thread is coming out of a cross-wise bead in the tubing ring. Zip the two pieces together by sewing from a cross-wise bead in the tubing through a cross-wise bead in the main bugle (**figure 11**). Do your best to center the tubing between the bell and the mouthpiece. Sew through 11 beads in the main bugle. If you feel the tube is too rounded at the bottom, stitch two rows of a few 11⁰s or 15⁰s between crosswise beads on the inside curve of the tube ring. Make sure that these extra beads frame a line of beads that lie lengthwise along the tube

(**figure 12**). Make sure that the tube isn't twisted when you start. End the threads.

6 Use the awl to help you place the knots where you want them. Cut the red string into two equal pieces. Tie them together with two knots, each knot 1¾ in. (4.4cm) from the center. String three 8⁰ seed beads onto both strings, and slide them to the knot. Tie a knot directly below the three beads. Repeat on the other end of the cords. Hold one knot directly against the base of the bell and tie another knot directly opposite the first knot. Tie the other end of the strings next to the mouthpiece in the same way. String a crystal, an 11⁰, a fire-polished bead, and an 11⁰ onto each end of the strings. Decide how low you'd like them to hang, and tie a knot to hold them in place. Trim each string about a ¼ in. (6mm) below the knots. Cut the ribbon into three equal pieces. Tie one at each end of the main bugle on the inside of the strings. Tie the third ribbon to the round tubing.

ANGEL FAIRY

Angels and fairies go with Christmas the way cake goes with birthdays. I think we love the idea of these flying spirits because we'd all like to be able to fly like one. And who couldn't use a guardian at some time in their life? Perhaps one of these guardian spirits will make someone, someday, feel blessed.

NOTE The step-up beads are marked with an "X" in the illustration. Refer to tubular peyote, p. 8, especially the section on adding thread.

HALO

Stretch and condition 2 ft. (61cm) of thread. Pick up 5 color E 15º seed beads. Sew through them again, leaving a 6-in. (15cm) tail **(figure 1, black outlines)**. Pick up an E, and sew through the next E. Repeat this stitch four times. Step up through the first E you picked up this round **(pink outlines)**. Pick up two Es, and sew through one E five times. Step up through the first E in the first pair you picked up **(blue outlines)**. Pick up an E, and sew through an E ten times. Step up through the first E you picked up **(yellow outlines)**. Pick up a color A 11º seed bead, and sew through an E ten times **(pink circles)**. End the threads. Set aside.

Supplies

- **1** 12mm glass pearl (white)
- **1** 6mm fire-polished bead (crystal)
- **1** 6mm heishi or 8mm star heishi bead (gold)
- **2** 4mm gold heishi beads (gold)
- 11º seed beads
  - **30** color A (gold)
  - **4.5g** color B (silver-lined crystal AB)
- 15º seed beads
  - **8.25g** color C (white-lined crystal AB)
  - **1.25g** color D (gold)
  - **7g** color E (silver-lined crystal)
- **1** 2-in. (5cm) 22- or 20-gauge headpin (gold)
- Toho One-G, Miyuki K-O, or C-Lon AA thread
- Size 10 and 12 beading needles
- Conditioner
- Thread snips
- Roundnose pliers
- Chainnose pliers
- Flush cutters

figure 1

- 11º seed beads, halo and wings (color A, gold)
- 11º seed beads, body (color B, silver-lined crystal AB)
- 11º seed beads, wings (color B, silver-lined crystal AB)
- 1º seed beads, wings (color C, white-lined crystal AB)
- 15º seed beads, wings (color D, gold)
- 15º seed beads, halo (color E, silver-lined crystal)

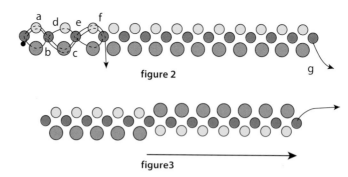

figure 2

figure3

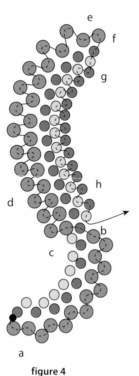

figure 4

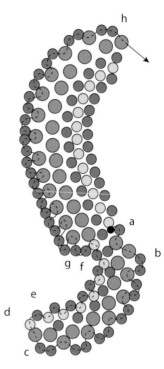

figure 5

WINGS

1 Stretch and condition 1 yd. (.9m) plus 6 in. (15cm) of thread. Pick up a color E 15º seed bead, a D, an E, and a color B 11º seed bead. Slide them to 12 in. (30cm) from the end of the thread, and sew through the E, D and E again **(figure 2, a–b)**.

2 Pick up a B, E, and D, and sew through the D at the end of the first cell and through the new B and E you picked up **(c–d–e)**. Pick up a D, E, and B, and sew through the E at the end of the previous cell and the D and B you picked up **(f)**. Repeat this step until you have 13 cells End with your thread coming out of the last E picked up **(g)**.

3 Pick up an D, E, and B, and sew through the E at the end of the last cell and through the D and E just picked up. Pick up a B, E, and D, and sew through the end E and the B and E you just picked up. Repeat this step until you have stitched seven cells. Finish by sewing through the end F **(figure 3)**.

4 Pick up a B, and sew through a B seven times **(figure 4, a–b)**. Continue through the next E and B **(c)**. Pick up a B, and sew through a B twelve times **(d–e)**. Pick up a B, and sew through an E and a D **(f)**. Pick up an E, and sew through a D twelve times **(g–h)**.

5 Pick up an E, and sew through two Bs **(figure 5, a)**. Pick up two Es, and sew through a B six times **(b-c)**. Pick up a D, and sew through an E and a D **(d)**. Pick up an E, and sew through a D six times **(e–f)**. Pick up two Es, and sew through a B 13 times **(g–h)**.

6 Sew through two Bs and a D to get back to the outside of the big curve **(figure 6, a)**. Pick up an E, and sew through two Es (the Es you are picking up go between the Es that were picked up as pairs at the end of step 5). Sew in 10 Es **(b–c)**. Pick up an E, and sew through an E, two Bs, an D, E, D, two Bs, and an E. Pick up an E, and sew through two Es **(d–e–f)**.

7 Pick up an E, A, and E, and sew through the center or point E in the next group of three Es. Do this nine times **(figure 7, a-b)**. Pick up an E, A, and E, and sew through two Es **(c)**. Sew along the inner curve until you sew through the pair of Es that sit where the curve starts to reverse and get larger **(d–e)**. Thread a needle onto the tail, and sew through a the outside B and E. Do not trim the thread or the tail. Make a second wing. Set them aside.

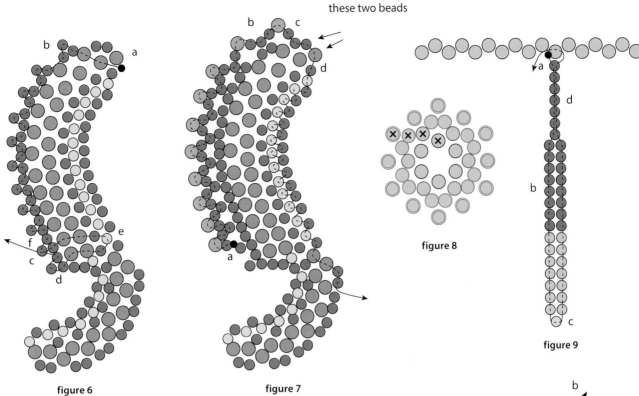

figure 6

figure 7

figure 8

figure 9

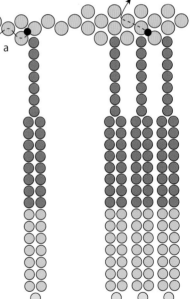

figure 10

sew tail through
these two beads

BODY

> **NOTE** Review the section on making a wrapped loop, p. 11, if needed. Step-up beads in the illustration are marked with an "X."

1 Stretch and condition 2½ yd. (2.3m) of thread. Pick up six Bs, slide them to 6 in. (15cm) from the end of the thread, and sew through them again. Sew through the first B again **(figure 8, black outlines)**. Pick up a B, and sew through a B six times. Step up through the first B you picked up. Pick up two Bs, and sew through a B six times **(blue outlines)**. Step up through a B.

2 Pick up a B, and sew through a B 12 times **(yellow outlines)**. Step up through a B. Repeat five or six times. Keep your tension firm so that the sides begin to draw up and make a tube. Secure the tail at this time, and trim the excess thread. On the headpin, string a 4mm heishi, the halo, the 12mm bead, a 4mm heishi and the 6mm star heishi. Slide the headpin through the center hole in the body so the head sits on the flat part and the pin goes through the inside. Slide the fire-polished bead onto the headpin, and make a wrapped loop.

Make it snug so that the head sits firmly on top of the body. Continue working in tubular peyote until the body is about 1½ in. (3.8cm) long. Secure the thread, but do not trim it. You will need to know where it is.

SKIRT

1 Stretch and condition 2 yd. (1.8m) of thread. Secure the thread in the body and exit a B at the very bottom edge.

2 Pick up 15 color C 15° seed beads, seven Es, a D, seven Es, and eight Cs, and sew through the first seven Cs and the B your thread exited at the start of this step **(figure 9, a–b–c–d–e)**.

3 Pick up a B, and sew through a B.

4 Repeat steps 2–3 11 times. Step up through a B to reach the next row in the skirt **(figure 10, a–b)**.

5 Repeat steps 2–4 to sew two more skirt layers. For these rows (and all future rows), sew through two Bs already in the body instead of picking up a B and sewing through a B as you move around the form. After a row in the skirt is finished, only sew through one bead to get to the next row. The next six rows of skirt begin decreasing the number of Cs in the first group of Cs you pick up — the counts of the D, Es, and the second group of C counts remain the same (see **figure 11**).

Row 1: Pick up 14 Cs and sew back through six **(a)**.

Row 2: Pick up 13 Cs and sew back through five **(b)**.

Row 3: Pick up 12 Cs and sew back through four **(c)**.

Row 4: Pick up 11 Cs and sew back through three **(d)**.

Row 5: Pick up 10 Cs and sew back through two **(e)**.

Row 6: Pick up nine Cs and sew back through one **(f)**. After row 6, secure the thread but do not trim it yet. You need to know where it is when you attach the wings.

ATTACH THE WINGS

Thread a needle on the thread exiting an E at the top of the wing. Sew through two body beads right where the body begins to form a tube **(figure 12)**. Sew through an E and a B. Sew through the two body beads and the wing beads again to strengthen the connection. Sew down to the bead indicated **(red outline)**. Use eight 15º seed beads of your choice to sew a loop to this bead. Sew through the loop a couple of times to strengthen it, and end the thread. Sew the other wing in place in the same way. Use the threads at the bottoms of the wings to connect those two Es to the body a couple of rows above the skirt. The placement will vary, depending on how sharply your wing curves and the way the wings shape themselves around the angel fairy's body.

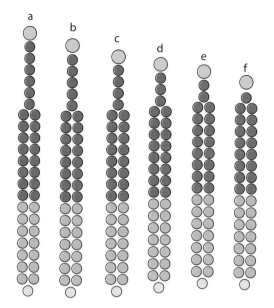

figure 11

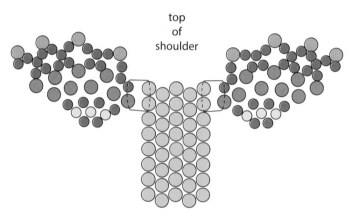

figure 12

on the back

70

GIFT BAGS

Presents are not the most important part of Christmas, but they ARE a fun part. These little bags will give pleasure year after year. If you have a special announcement to make or question to ask, you could write it on a piece of paper and present it in one of these bags for a little extra flair. There's even a birthday design for all the December and early January babies whose birthdays get lost in the holiday shuffle.

NOTE **BEAD QUANTITIES**

As noted below, the Christmas gift bags require 4g of color A 11º cylinder beads, 3.5g of color B 11º cylinder beads, and 1.75g of color C 11º cylinder beads.

The birthday bag requires 4g of color A, 3.5g of color B, .25g of color C and color D 11º cylinder beads, and 1g of color E 11º cylinder beads.

The tissue paper is an optional part of the gift bag. The diamond pattern requires an additional 4.5g of color A, 3.25g of color B, and .75g of color C. You will need 1.5g of 11º seed beads. The diagonal paper requires 3.75g of colors A, B, and C, as well as 1.5g of 11º seed beads.

Review the section on increasing and decreasing for diagonal peyote on pp. 9-10 and tubular peyote, p. 8.

BAG BODY

1 **All bags:** Stretch and condition a comfortable length of thread. Pick up 64 color A 11º cylinder beads. Sew through all the beads again, and continue through the first bead one more time. The boxes marked with red outlines indicate the first bead of each new row **(patterns 1 and 2)**. This bead is also your step-up bead.
Christmas bag: Stitch two rows of peyote stitch using only As. Don't forget to step up. The first non-A bead you pick up will be the color B 11º cylinder bead marked with an "X".
Birthday bag: Stitch only one row of

Supplies

PURPLE GIFT BAG
- 11º cylinder beads
  - **4g** color A (silver-lined dyed purple)
  - **3.5g** color B (light lemon ice yellow)
  - **1.75g** color C (opaque chartreuse)
- **.5g** 15º seed beads (yellow-lined crystal AB)
- Toho One-G, K-O thread, C-Lon AA, or an equivalent for the bag,
- Size D thread or an equivalent for the tissue paper
- Sizes 10 and 12 needles
- Conditioner
- Thread snips
- Cardboard tube

TRADITIONAL CHRISTMAS COLORS
- 11º cylinder beads
  - Color A: opaque white
  - Color B: matte dark red
  - Color C: metallic green
- 11º seed beads: opaque white, matte red, or metallic green
- 15º seed beads: white-lined crystal AB

BIRTHDAY BAG
- 11º cylinder beads
  - Color A: matte black
  - Color B: cream ceylon
  - Color C: opaque red AB
  - Color D: salmon pink ceylon
  - Color E: dyed opaque maroon
- 11º seed beads: black AB
- 15º seed beads: jet-lined crystal

peyote using A beads. The first non-A bead you pick up will the B marked with an "X."

2 Cut the cardboard tube so you can roll it into a tighter cylinder. Slide the tube through the peyote ring so it provides a form for you to stitch around **(photo a)**. You can tape the tube to help it hold its shape. Continue reading the chart until you reach the top. After you complete the top row, sew through one of the beads marked by a "handles" arrow. Pick up 35 15º seed beads. Sew through the other handle bead on the same face of the bag. Sew back through the 15ºs and the "handle" bead in the bag again. Sew back through the 15ºs and the second handle bead. Stitch along the top to the next bead indicated by an arrow, and repeat for a second handle. End the threads.

3 Check the placement of the "bottom" arrows. Stretch and condition 1 yd. (.9m) of thread. Add it to the beadwork, and bring it through any one of the bottom beads indicated. The arrows show the direction of the thread. Work peyote stitch with eight As. Do a turn-around stitch **(figure 1, red line)**. Stitch a row with only seven As. Stitch another row with eight As. Continue stitching rows of seven and eight beads. You'll have to

A

do a turn-around stitch at the end of the eight-bead rows. Stop when you have 19 rows. Attach the bottom to the other side by sewing into one of the beads that has an arrow coming out of it in the chart. Do a turn-around stitch, and zip the two sides together.

4 Continue sewing along the lower edge until you sew through one of the beads marked with a circle. Stitch a row of four beads. Turn around and stitch a row of three beads. Turn around and stitch a row with two beads. Turn around and stitch a single bead. Sew through one of the beads indicated by an arrow in **figure 2**. Turn around and

stitch back through the other bead with an arrow. Sew through the free end of the point bead point so that this bead is snugly against the two arrow beads. Stitch through these beads again. Stitch along the bottom edge of the bag to reach another bead marked with a circle on the other side of the bag. Make another triangle and attach it to the bottom. End the threads.

TISSUE PAPER: DIAMOND

NOTE A pair of single sections of either of these patterns would make a fantastic pair of earrings.

1 If you want to make the diamond tissue paper, refer to the instructions for the Abstract Bow, p. 41 and the instructions for "Diagonal peyote," p. 10. Switch to the chart on p. 74 as soon as you are comfortable with increasing and decreasing on the first half of the each piece. Note that when you stitch the second side, the first three increases share the 11ºs that were sewn in the first three increases on the first side **(figures 4 and 5)**. The next five increases on the second side have their own 11ºs. The last increase shares an 11º with the last increase on the first side. There are four panels in all. The first one is stitched as

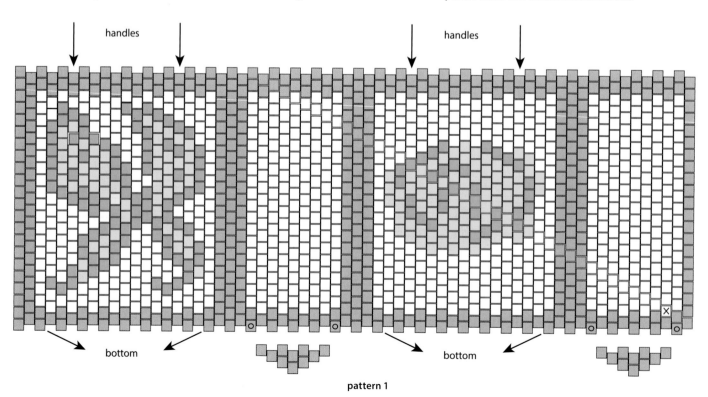

handles   handles

bottom   bottom

pattern 1

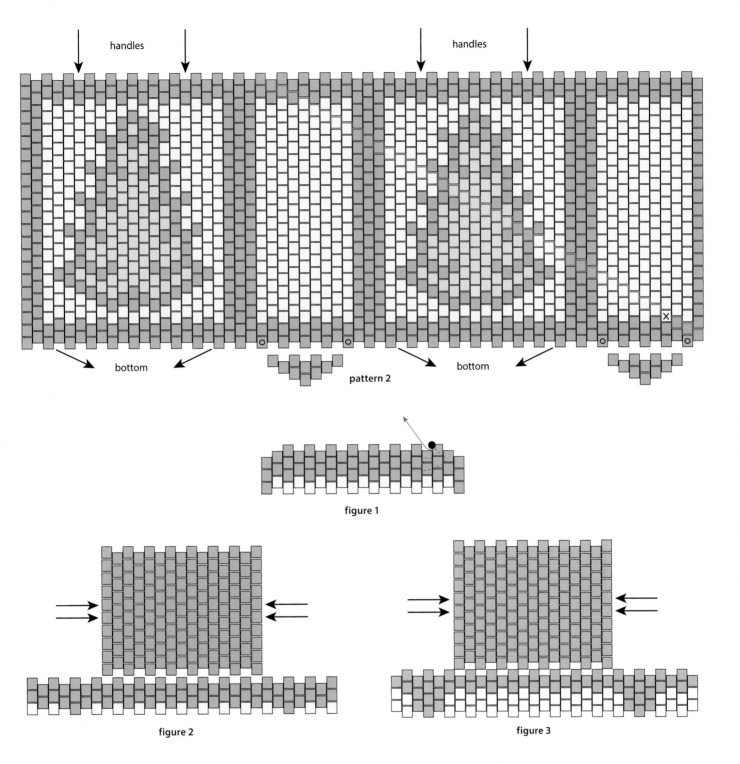

handles handles

bottom bottom

pattern 2

figure 1

figure 2

figure 3

shown in figure 5. Note that you fill in the pattern after the last increase stitch. Secure the thread after stitching the last C in place. Finish off the second side and secure the thread in the same way.

Second panel: Stitch the first side as you did for the first panel and secure the thread. Follow the chart to stitch the second side, but do not secure the thread. Instead, pick up an 11º and an A, and sew through a C **(figure 6, a)**. Continue working in peyote stitch as shown in **(b–c)**.

Line up the two panels so the "V"s are pointing the same way. Also, make sure the ridges made by the shared 11ºs are on the same side. Zip the second side to one of the sides on the first panel. Pick up an 11º after you sew through the last A. Sew through another A **(d–e)**. Secure the thread.

Third panel: Make a third panel exactly as you made the second panel.

Fourth panel: Do not secure either thread on the fourth panel. Finish off

both sides as shown in **figure 6**. Zip one side of the fourth panel to one of the sides of the three panels already zipped together. Roll the free ends together so the shared 11º increase beads are inside, and zip the remaining side together as shown. End the threads.

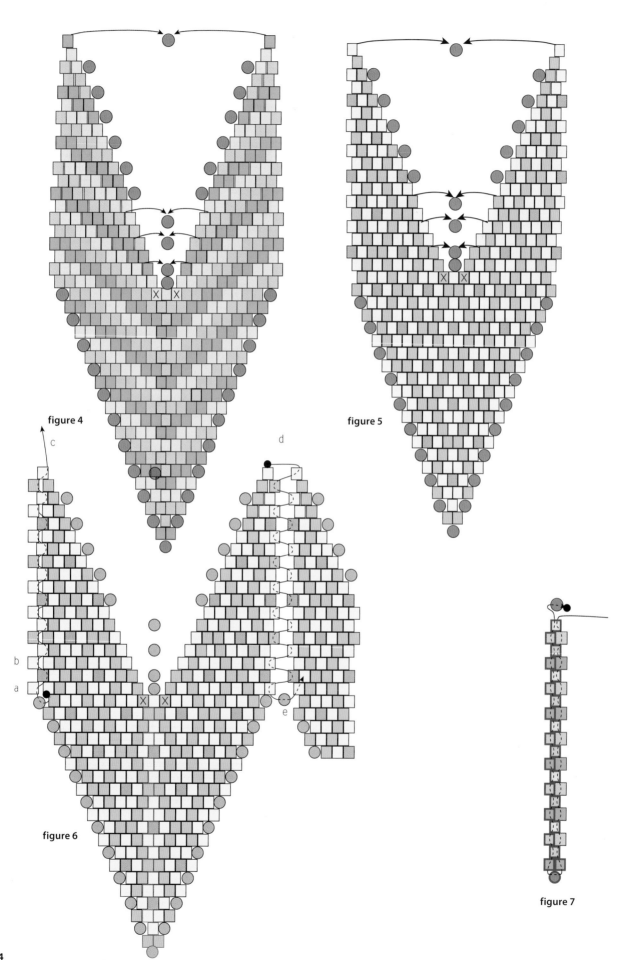

figure 4

figure 5

figure 6

figure 7

TISSUE PAPER: DIAGONAL

1 Review "Diagonal peyote," p. 9, if you are unfamiliar with this stitch. Stretch and condition 2 yd. (1.8m) of thread. String a stop bead, and center it on the thread. Pick up an A, two Bs, a C, an A, two Bs, a C, an A, two Bs, a C, an A, two Bs, a C, an 11º, and a C. These are the beads outlined in blue in **figure 7**. Sew back through the last B. Pick up a B, and sew through an A. Pick up a C, and sew through a B. Pick up a B, and sew through an A. Pick up a C, and sew through a B. Pick up a B, and sew through an A. Pick up a C, and sew through a B. Pick up a B, and sew through an A. Pick up a C, sew through a B, pick up a B, sew through an A. Pick up an 11º, and sew up and down through these three rows again. Stop when you exit the top A. Pick up an A represented by either bead marked with an "X" in **figure 8**. Follow the chart, and continue.

2 When you reach the bottom, work a decrease turn-around by picking up an 11º and a cylinder. Review the section on increasing and decreasing in diagonal peyote on p. 9. The color of the beads used will change, so refer to the chart when you reach a decrease turn-around. After you stitch back to the top, work an increase turn-around by picking up a cylinder, an 11º seed bead, and another cylinder. Sew back through the first cylinder bead you picked up. Refer to the chart to make sure you pick up the right beads. Make sure these beads are snug against the panel. Don't worry if the 11º and the second cylinders twist into each other's places — you will fix that with a future row.

3 First panel: Make the first panel as shown in **figure 4**. The first three increases of the second half connect to the 11ºs in the first three increases of the first half. The next six increases have their own 11ºs. The last increase shares the 11º with the last increase of the first half.

Second panel: Make one side as shown in **figure 4**. After you stitch the last B in place, sew through a few beads so that you can get turned around and come back out of the same bead heading back to the increase side. Peyote stitch an A, a C, an A, a C, an A, a C, an A, a C, and an A in place **(figure 7, a–b)**. End the thread. Stitch the second half, but do not secure the thread. Instead, zip this side to one in the first panel — make sure the shared beads are facing the same way. After you sew through the last B, pick up an 11º and sew through the facing B **(c–d)**. End the thread.

Third panel: Make a panel just like the first one. Zip one side to the free side of the second panel. Since you have to make sure the shared beads are all on the same side, check the first side before you trim the thread to see if this is the side you need to zip. You will pick up an 11º and zip from the bottom up as shown **(figure 9)**. Sew back down through the zip so that you catch that B where you started that didn't get zipped. End the thread.

Fourth panel: Follow step 3 to make the fourth panel. Zip each side to a free side of the paper. Check to make sure the shared increase 11ºs are on the inside. End the thread, and put the paper in the bag.

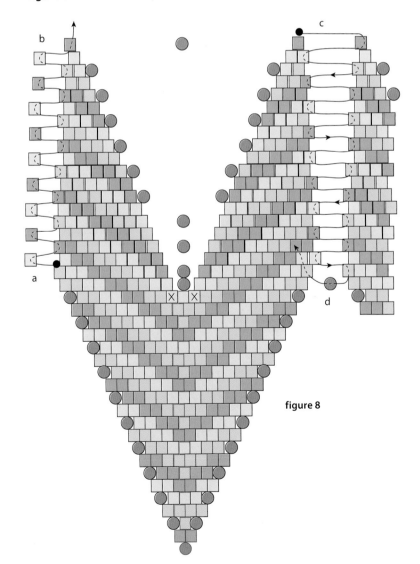

figure 8

figure 9

CHAPTER 5
Mini Ornament Covers

BUBBLING WITH JOY

Bubbles and fun go hand-in-hand, from the simple pleasure of blowing bubbles to the bliss of a bubble bath to the way a glass of champagne transforms any moment into a special occasion. Anyone who is lucky enough to receive one of these ornaments is sure to bubble with enthusiasm.

Supplies

CRYSTAL BLUE

- **1** 27mm glass ball ornament
- **6** 9x7mm fire-polished drops (crystal AB)
- **12** 6mm bicone beads (lilac)
- **6** 4mm crystal bicones (deep purple)
- **8g** 3.4mm Japanese drop seed beads (silver-lined crystal)
- **1.75g** 11º seed beads (blue iris)
- **1g** 15º seed beads (silver-lined light purple)
- **12** 6mm bead caps (silver)
- **12** 4mm bead caps (silver)
- Toho One-G or K-O thread

- Sizes 10 and 12 beading needles
- Conditioner
- Thread snips

RED BLUSH COLORS

- 9x7mm drops: crystal AB
- 6mm bicone beads: light amethyst
- 6mm bicones: crystal AB
- 4mm crystal bicones: light amethyst
- 3.4mm Japanese drop seed beads: merlot mix
- 11º seed beads: silver-lined crystal AB
- 15º seed beads: purple iris

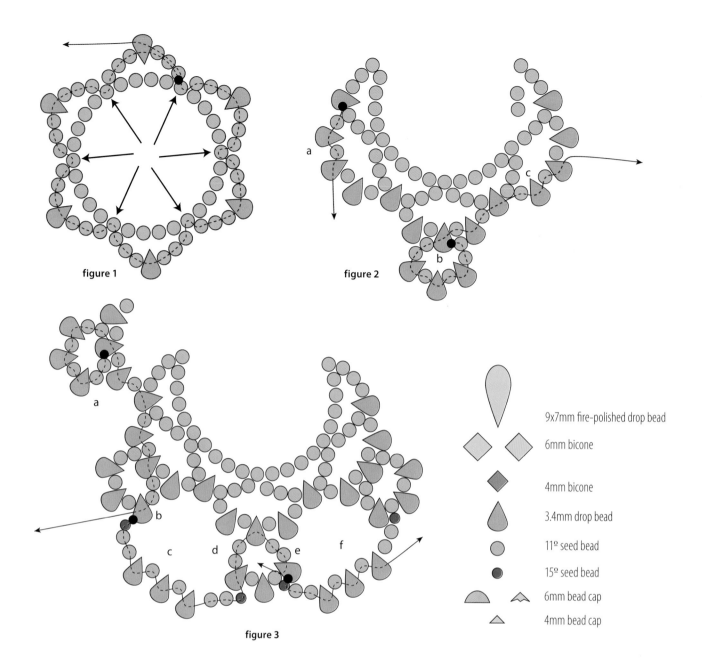

figure 1

figure 2

figure 3

9x7mm fire-polished drop bead

6mm bicone

4mm bicone

3.4mm drop bead

11º seed bead

15º seed bead

6mm bead cap

4mm bead cap

NOTE The key shows that the 6mm bead caps and the 6mm bicones are divided into two groups of six. If you choose to use two different 6mm caps and two different colors of 6mm bicones, use one kind of bead cap and one color with the 9x7 drops and the other caps and bicones with the 4mm bicones.

1 Stretch and condition 2½ yd. (2.29m) of thread. Thread a needle. Pick up 30 11º seed beads. Sew through all the beads again, leaving a 15-in. (38cm) tail. Sew once more through the first bead. Pick up three 11ºs, a 3.4mm drop, and three 11ºs, skip four beads, and sew through the fifth 11ºin the ring. Repeat this stitch for a total of six swags of three

11ºs, a drop, and three 11ºs. Continue through three 11ºs and a drop **(figure 1)**.

2 Pick up an 11º, a 3.4mm a drop, an 11º, a drop, an 11º, a drop, and an 11º, and sew through the drop in the next swag. Sew six of these swags in place. Continue through an 11º, drop, 11º, and drop **(figure 2, a)**. Pick up two 11ºs, a drop, an 11º, a drop, an 11º, a drop, and two 11ºs, and sew through the center drop in the swag so the beads you picked up form a little loop below it. Continue through an 11º, drop, 11º, drop, 11º, drop, 11º, and drop **(b, c)**. Sew six little loops. After you finish the sixth loop, continue sewing to the swag that has the first loop. Sew through the cen-

ter drop in the swag and two 11ºs and the first drop in the little loop **(figure 3, a–b)**. Pick up a 15º seed bead, two 11ºs, a drop, an 11º, a drop, an 11º, a drop, two 11ºs, and a 15º, and sew through a drop, two 11ºs, drop, two 11ºs, and drop in the next loop **(c–e)**. Repeat around to connect the loops in the same manner. After you finish the sixth swag, continue through a 15º, two 11ºs, drop, 11º, drop, 11º, and drop **(f)**.

3 Pick up three 15ºs, and sew through the center drop in the small loop **(figure 4, a)**. Pick up three 15ºs, and sew through the drop, 11º, drop, 11º, and drop **(b–c)**. Repeat around. After you sew the twelfth group of three 15ºs in place, continue through a single 15º.

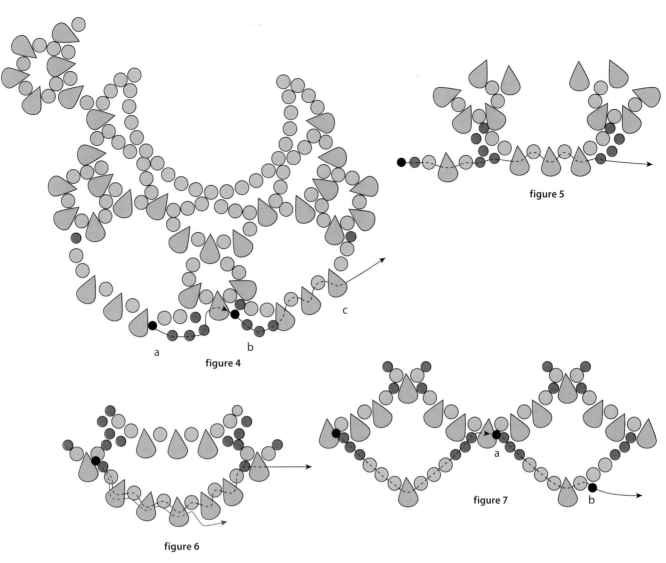

figure 5

figure 4

figure 6

figure 7

figure 8

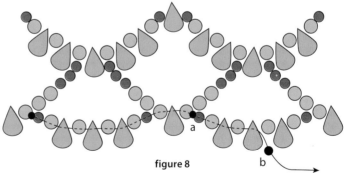

4 Pick up a 15º, 11º, drop, 11º, and 15º, and sew through a 15º, drop, 11º, drop, 11º, drop, and 15º **(figure 5)**. Sew six of these swags in place, and continue through a 15º, 11º, and drop in the first swag you sewed in place. Pick up a 15º, 11º, drop, 11º, drop, 11º, drop, 11º, drop, 11º, drop, 11º, and 15º, and sew through the drop in a 15º, 11º, drop, 11º, and 15º swag **(figure 6, black dotted line)**. Repeat around. After the sixth swag is sewn in place, continue through a 15º, 11º, drop, 11º, drop, 11º, and drop of a long swag **(red dotted line)**.

5 Pick up three 15ºs, three 11ºs, a drop, three 11ºs, and three 15ºs, and sew through the center drop in the swag

with five drops **(figure 7, a)**. Repeat around. After the sixth swag, continue through three 15ºs, three 11ºs, a drop, and an 11º **(b)**. Pick up a 15º, an 11º, a drop, an 11º, a drop, an 11º, a drop, an 11º, and a 15º, and sew through the center 11º, drop, and 11º of the next swag **(figure 8, a)**. Repeat around. After you have sewn the sixth swag, continue through a 15º, 11º, drop, 11º, and drop **(b)**.

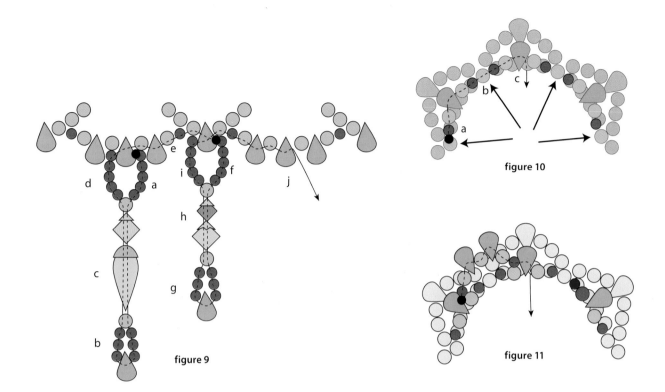

figure 9

figure 10

figure 11

6 Make the dangles: Pick up five 15⁰s, an 11⁰, a 4mm bead cap, a 6mm bicone, a 6mm bead cap, a 9x7mm crystal drop, an 11⁰, three 15⁰s, a drop, and three 15⁰s **(figure 9, a–b)**. Sew back through the last 11⁰, 9x7mm drop, 6mm bead cap, 6mm bicone, 4mm bead cap, and 11⁰. Pick up five 15⁰s, and sew through a drop, 11⁰, drop, 11⁰, 15⁰, 11⁰, and drop **(c–e)**. Pick up five 15⁰s, an 11⁰, a 4mm bead cap, a 4mm bicone, a 6mm bead cap, a 6mm bicone, an 11⁰, three 15⁰s, a drop, and three 15⁰s **(f, g)**, and sew back through an 11⁰, 6mm bicone, 6mm bead cap, 4mm bicone, 4mm bead cap, and 11⁰. Pick up five 15⁰s, and sew through a drop, 11⁰, 15⁰, 11⁰, drop, 11⁰, and drop **(h–j)**. Repeat this step until you have 12 dangles sewn in place. End the thread.

7 Thread a needle onto the tail. Refer to **figure 1** again. Make sure the thread is exiting any one of the beads that has an arrow pointing to it. Pick up a 15⁰, an 11⁰, a drop, an 11⁰, and a 15⁰, skip four 11⁰s, and sew through the fifth **(figure 10, a–b)**. Repeat around. Continue through a 15⁰, 11⁰, and drop **(c)**. Pick up a 15⁰, an 11⁰, a drop, an 11⁰, a drop, an 11⁰, and a 15⁰. Sew through the drop in the next swag **(figure 11)**. Repeat around. End the thread.

Supplies

GREEN ORNAMENT

- **1** 28mm glass ball ornament
- **25** 7.5mm two-hole ginkgo leaf beads (luster opaque green)
- **10** 5x7mm fire-polished drops (green iris)
- **5** 4mm fire-polished beads (halo madder rose)
- **15** 3mm melon beads (luster iris sapphire)
- **10** 2mm fire-polished beads (french rose)
- **.75g** 11º seed beads (galvanized pink lilac)
- **2g** 15º seed beads (ceylon celery green)
- **1.5g** 11º Demi seed beads (jonquil-lined lined crystal)
- Toho One-G thread or K-O thread
- Sizes 10 and 12 beading needles
- Stop bead
- Conditioner
- Thread snips

LONGEVITY

The ginkgo leaf has long been a favorite motif for designs because of its unusual, balanced shape. We are lucky that there is finally a ginkgo bead perfect for beadweaving! As a symbol, it often means longevity, and one of these ornaments can be a long-lived reminder of your good thoughts.

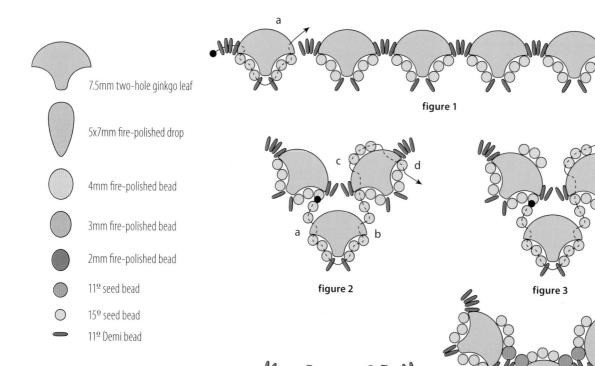

figure 1

figure 2

figure 3

figure 4

figure 5

Legend

7.5mm two-hole ginkgo leaf

5x7mm fire-polished drop

4mm fire-polished bead

3mm fire-polished bead

2mm fire-polished bead

11º seed bead

15º seed bead

11º Demi bead

NOTE Always pick up the ginkgo leaves from the broad, domed side.

FIRST HALF

1 Stretch and condition 1 yd. (.9m) of thread. String a stop bead, and slide it to 8 in. (20cm) from the end of the thread. Pick up four 11º Demi beads, a ginkgo bead, three 15º seed beads, two Demis, and three 15ºs, and sew through the free hole in the ginkgo **(figure 1, a)**. Repeat this step four times. Continue through the first four Demis, ginkgo, and 15º **(b)**.

2 Pick up two 15ºs, a ginkgo, three 15ºs, two Demis, and three 15ºs, and sew through the free hole of the ginkgo **(figure 2, a–b)**. Pick up two 15ºs, and sew through the first 15º adjacent to the next ginkgo and the ginkgo **(b–c)**. Pick up three 15ºs, and sew through a ginkgo and a 15º. Pick up three 15ºs, and sew through the other hole of the ginkgo and a 15º **(figure 2)**. Repeat this step four times. Continue sewing through beads until you sew through three 15ºs in the center ring **(figure 3)**. Pick up an 11º seed bead, and sew through the center two Demis. Pick up an 11º, and sew through three 15ºs **(figure 4, a)**. Repeat these stitches along the inside ring. When done, end the thread and tail in the center ring of 11ºs and 15ºs.

3 Stretch and condition 1 yd. (.9m) of thread. String a stop bead, and slide it to 8 in. (20cm) from the end of the thread. Sew through a 15º and ginkgo in one of the lower leaves **(b)**. *Pick up four 15ºs and sew through the other hole of the ginkgo and a 15º **(c–d)**. Pick up a 15º, an 11º, a 15º, a ginkgo, three 15ºs, two Demis, and three 15ºs, and sew through the free hole in the ginkgo. Pick up a 15º, an 11º, and a 15º, and sew through a 15º and the next ginkgo* **(figure 5)**. Repeat the sequence between asterisks until you get back to the beginning. After you sew through the last 15º and ginkgo, continue through four 15ºs, a ginkgo, three 15ºs, and a Demi **(figure 6)**.

4 Pick up two 15ºs, a Demi, an 11º, a 3mm fire-polished bead, an 11º, a Demi, the drop bead, and a 15º, and sew back through a drop, Demi, 11º, 3mm, 11º, Demi, and two 15ºs **(figure 7, a)**. Continue through a Demi and two 15ºs,

skip a 15º, and continue through a 15º, 11º, 15º, ginkgo, three 15ºs, two Demis, three 15ºs, ginkgo, 15º, 11º, and 15º. Skip a 15º, and sew through two 15ºs and a Demi **(b–c–d–e)**. Repeat this step four times. After you have sewn through the last 15º, 11º, and 15º, end the threads in the ginkgos in the middle row. Do not place any knots in the lowest or widest row of beads. Set this half of the cover aside.

SECOND HALF

1 Stretch and condition 1 yd. (.9m) of thread. String a stop bead, and slide it to 8 in. (20cm) from the end of the thread. Pick up a Demi, a ginkgo, three 15ºs, two Demis, and three 15ºs, and sew through the free hole in the ginkgo. Repeat until you have five ginkgos sewn together. Continue through a Demi, ginkgo, three 15ºs, two Demis, three 15ºs, and a ginkgo.

figure 6

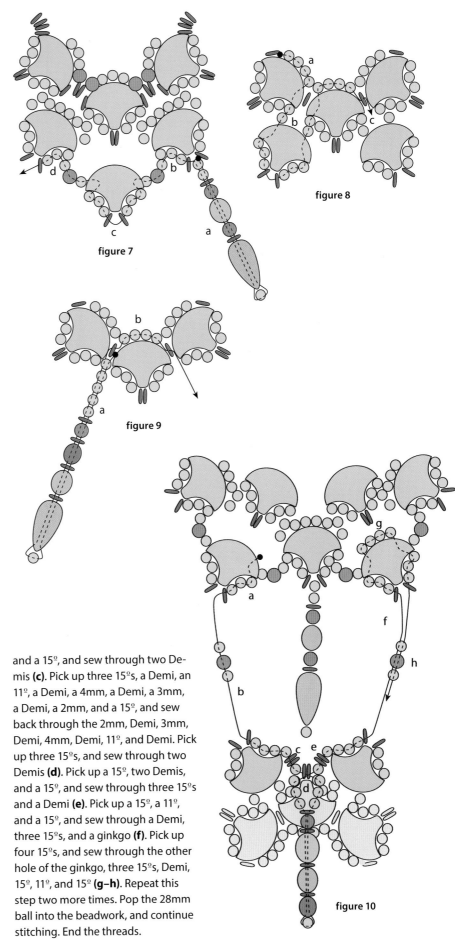

figure 7

figure 8

figure 9

figure 10

2 Pick up four 15ºs, and sew through the other hole in the ginkgo and a 15º **(figure 8, a)**. Pick up a 15º, a ginkgo, three 15ºs, two Demis, and three 15ºs, and sew through the free hole in the ginkgo. Pick up a 15º, and sew through a 15º and a ginkgo **(b)**. Repeat this step until you have sewn on four more ginkgos. After you have sewn through the last 15º and ginkgo, continue through four 15ºs and a Demi **(c)**.

3 Pick up five 15ºs, a Demi, a 11º, a Demi, a 2mm fire-polished bead, a Demi, a 3mm, a Demi, a drop, and a 15º, and sew back through the drop, Demi, 3mm, Demi, 2mm, Demi, 11º, Demi, and five 15ºs **(figure 9, a)**. Make sure your tension isn't too tight. Continue through a Demi, four 15ºs, and a Demi **(b)**. Repeat this step until you have sewn on five dangles. Sew through just the five groups of four 15ºs. End the threads anywhere in the center ginkgos. Do not secure them or leave a loose thread in any of the Demis or 15ºs.

FINISH

1 Stretch and condition 1 yd. (.9m) of thread. String on a stop bead, and slide it to 8 in. (20cm) from the end of the thread. Pick up the first half of the cover that has three rows of ginkgos, and sew through a hole in a ginkgo that does not have any 15ºs along the broad curve. Continue through three 15ºs and a Demi **(figure 10, a)**. Pick up a 15º, an 11º, and a 15º.

2 Sew through a Demi and three 15ºs in the outer row of ginkgos in the second half **(b)**. Pick up a 15º, two Demis,

and a 15º, and sew through two Demis **(c)**. Pick up three 15ºs, a Demi, an 11º, a Demi, a 4mm, a Demi, a 3mm, a Demi, a 2mm, and a 15º, and sew back through the 2mm, Demi, 3mm, Demi, 4mm, Demi, 11º, and Demi. Pick up three 15ºs, and sew through two Demis **(d)**. Pick up a 15º, two Demis, and a 15º, and sew through three 15ºs and a Demi **(e)**. Pick up a 15º, a 11º, and a 15º, and sew through a Demi, three 15ºs, and a ginkgo **(f)**. Pick up four 15ºs, and sew through the other hole of the ginkgo, three 15ºs, Demi, 15º, 11º, and 15º **(g–h)**. Repeat this step two more times. Pop the 28mm ball into the beadwork, and continue stitching. End the threads.

BLUE/PURPLE ORNAMENT COVER

- **1** 28mm glass ball ornament

- **25** 16x5mm two-hole daggers (matte metallic flax)

- **10** 5mm mini tile beads (pastel bordeaux)

- **55** 4mm mini Es-O beads (light pearl blue)

- **25** 4mm fire-polished beads (light sapphire)

- **25** 3mm fire-polished beads (light sapphire)

- **30** 2mm fire-polished beads (light sapphire)

- 11º seed beads

  - **1.75g** color A (matte gold)

  - **2.25g** color B (purple suede)

- **3.75g** 15º seed beads (blue iris)

- Toho One-G thread or Miyuki K-O thread

- Sizes 10 and 12 beading needles

- Stop beads

- Conditioner

- Thread snips

OLIVINE/TOPAZ ORNAMENT COLORS

- 16x5mm two-hole daggers: topaz luster

- 5mm mini tile beads: pastel olivine

- 4mm mini Es-O beads: cream

- 4mm fire-polished beads: olivine

- 3mm fire-polished beads: olivine

- 2mm fire-polished beads: sueded gold lamé

- 11º seed beads

  - Color A: silver-lined root beer

  - Color B: metallic gold iris

- 15º seed beads: transparent chartreuse AB

ALL ABOUT THE FRINGE

Fabulous fringe: You can't have too much of it! It's a simple technique — and an often underappreciated one — that adds a lot of pizzazz to anything it embellishes. Sometimes it's regarded as a bit old-fashioned or dated. Instead, just think of it as retro. You'll love the drape it gives this ornament cover.

ORNAMENT COVER

1 Stretch and condition 1 yd. (.9m) of thread. Pick up a mini Es-O bead, a 15º seed bead, a color A 11º seed bead, a 2mm fire-polished bead, an A, and a 15º five times. Tie a knot. Sew through the first Es-O again, and continue through the free hole in the Es-O (**figure 1**). Pick up a 15º, a mini tile bead, and a 15º, and sew through the free hole in the next Es-O. (**figure 2, a**). Repeat four times. Continue through a 15º and a tile (**b**).

2 Pick up three 15ºs, and sew through the free hole in the tile. Pick up three 15ºs, and sew through the other hole of the same tile, and the following 15º, Es-O, 15º, and tile (**figure 3**). Repeat these stitches four times. Continue through the first three 15ºs added to the first tile. Pick up three 15ºs, a tile, and three 15ºs, and sew through the next three 15ºs, tile, and three 15ºs (**figure 4**). Repeat this stitch four times. End the threads.

3 Stretch and condition 2 yd. (1.8m) of thread. String a stop bead, and slide it to 6 in. (15cm) from the end of the thread. Sew through a free hole in a tile. Pick up a 15º, an A an Es-O, an A, an Es-O, an A, an Es-O, an A, and a 15º, and sew through the free hole in the next tile. Connect the five tiles with this sequence. After you have sewn through the fifth tile, continue through the next 15º and A (**figure 5, a**). *Pick up two 15ºs, and sew through the free hole in the Es-O (**b**). Pick up an A, and sew through the free hole in an Es-O twice (**c**). Pick up two 15ºs, and sew through an A (**d**). Pick up two 15ºs, an A, an Es-O, and three 15ºs, and sew through the free hole in the Es-O (**e**). Pick up three 15ºs, and sew through the other hole in the Es-O (**f**). Pick up an A and two 15ºs, and sew through the next A (**g**).* Repeat the sequence between the asterisks four times. When done, continue sewing through beads until you sew through

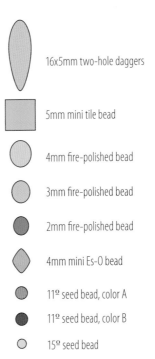

16x5mm two-hole daggers

5mm mini tile bead

4mm fire-polished bead

3mm fire-polished bead

2mm fire-polished bead

4mm mini Es-O bead

11º seed bead, color A

11º seed bead, color B

15º seed bead

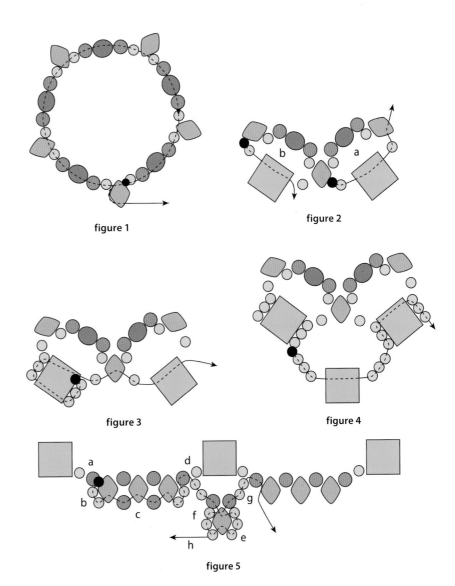

figure 1

figure 2

figure 3

figure 4

figure 5

three 15ºs, an Es-O, and a 15º in one of the Es-Os you sewed into place during this step **(h)**.

4 Pick up A, Es-O, A, Es-O, A, Es-O, A, Es-O, A, Es-O, A, Es-O, and two 15ºs. Sew through the free hole in the end Es-O **(figure 6, a)**. Pick up a color B 11º seed bead and sew through the free hole of the next Es-O five times **(b)**. Pick up two 15ºs and sew through an Es-O, A, Es-O, A, Es-O, A, Es-O, A, and Es-O **(c)**. Pick up an A, and sew through the next 15º, Es-O, and 15º **(d)**. Repeat this step four times, and end the thread.

5 Stretch and condition 2 yd. (1.8m) of thread. String a stop bead and slide it to 6 in. (15cm) from the end. Sew through an Es-O and B. *Pick up seven 15ºs, an A, three Bs, an A, a B, a 2mm, an A, a 3mm, an A, a 4mm, an A, a B, three 15ºs, the top hole of a two-hole dagger, and three 15ºs **(figure 7, a)**. Pick up three 15ºs, and sew through the other hole in the dagger **(b)**. Pick up three 15ºs, and sew through the top hole in the dagger **(c)**. Pick up three 15ºs, and sew back through the B, A, 4mm, A, 3mm, A, 2mm, B, and A **(d)**. Pick up three Bs, and sew through an A. Pick up seven 15ºs, and sew through the B your thread exited at the start of the fringe and the next Es-O and B **(e–f)**. Sew a fringe dangle to each B. After you have picked up the second set of seven 15ºs in the fifth dangle, sew through a B and an Es-O. Pick up a B, and sew through an Es-O and a B* **(g)**. Repeat the sequence between asterisks five times. End the threads.

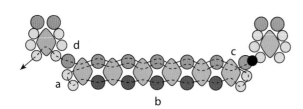

figure 6

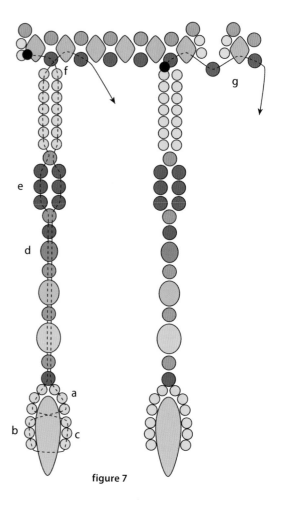

figure 7

Supplies

REGAL BLUE COVER

- **1** 28mm glass ball ornament
- **7** 12x9mm crystal drops (light sapphire)
- **7** 6mm bicone crystals in each of 2 colors (light amethyst and light sapphire)
- **7** 4mm bicone crystals (light sapphire)
- **7** 3mm crystal pearls (light blue)
- **35** two-hole lentil beads (Czech-mates light blue pearl coat)
- **28** MiniDuo beads (amethyst luster)
- **2.25g** berry beads (purple-lined crystal)
- **1g** 11º seed beads, (silver-lined smoky amethyst AB)
- 15º seed beads
  - **3g** color A (blue iris)
  - **.5g** color B (silver-lined light purple)
- **7** 8mm bead caps (silver)
- **14** 6mm bead caps (silver)
- **7** 4mm bead caps (silver)
- Toho One-G, K-O, or C-Lon AA thread
- Sizes 10 and 12 beading needles
- Stop beads
- Conditioner
- Thread snips

HEATHER COVER COLORS

- 12x9mm crystal drops: rosaline
- 6mm bicone crystals: erinite and amethyst
- 4mm bicone crystals: amethyst
- 3mm crystal pearls: light peach
- two-hole lentils: luster-opaque amethyst
- MiniDuo beads: pastel olivine
- berry beads: transparent gray rainbow luster
- 11º seed beads: green iris
- 15º seed beads
  - Color A: purple iris
  - Color B: silver-lined olivine

RESPLENDENT

The rich texture of this opulent cover evokes the craftsmanship of artisans who catered to the tastes of imperial courtiers. Almost everyone who sees it stops to take a closer look at the detailing. Don't be surprised if you keep one of these for yourself.

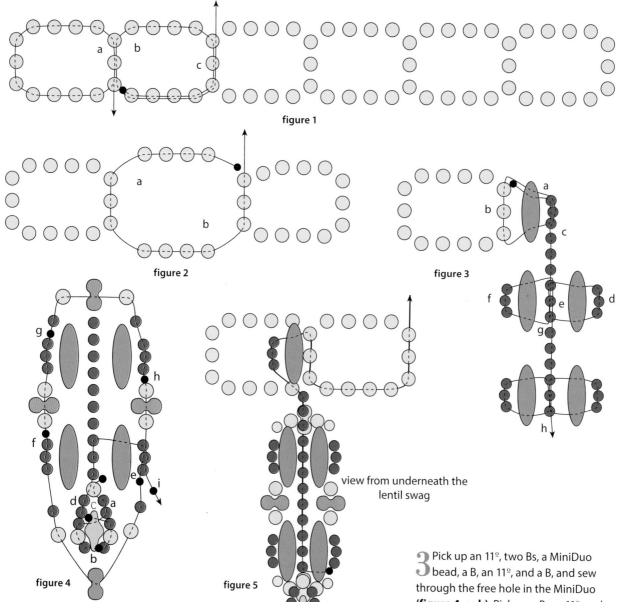

figure 1

figure 2

figure 3

figure 4

figure 5

view from underneath the
lentil swag

NOTE I do not recommend using
lentils that have a finish (such as AB) that is
only on one side the first time you make
this cover.

ORNAMENT COVER

1 Stretch and condition 7 ft. (2.13m) of
thread. String a stop bead and slide
it to 12 in. (30cm) from the end of the
thread. Pick up 14 11º seed beads, and
sew through the first three beads again
so the beads form a rectangle with four
beads on the top and bottom and three
beads on each side. The tail must exit
three side beads (**figure 1, a**). Pick up
11 11ºs, and sew through three side
beads and the first seven beads you
picked up to form a second rectangle
(**b–c**). Keep picking up 11 beads and
sewing rectangles until you have six

rectangles. Pick up four 11ºs, and sew
through the three 11ºs at the far end
of the strip. Pick up four 11ºs, and sew
through the opposite three 11ºs, to complete the rectangle (**figure 2**).

2 Pick up a lentil by either hole and
three color B 15º seed beads, and
sew through the free hole in the lentil.
Sew through the three side 15ºs, the
lentil, and the Bs (**figure 3, a–b–c**). *Pick
up six Bs, a lentil, and three Bs, and sew
through the free hole in the lentil and
the last three 15ºs of the group of six
you picked up (**d–e**). Pick up a lentil and
three Bs, and sew through the free hole
and the bottom three Bs again* (**f–g**).
Repeat the section between asterisks to
sew a second pair of lentils in place (**h**).

3 Pick up an 11º, two Bs, a MiniDuo
bead, a B, an 11º, and a B, and sew
through the free hole in the MiniDuo
(**figure 4, a–b**). Pick up a B, an 11º, and
a B, and sew through the other hole in
the MiniDuo (**c**). Pick up two Bs, and sew
back through an 11º, three Bs, lentil, and
three Bs (**d–e**). Pick up a B, an 11º, a berry
bead, an 11º, and a B, and sew through
three Bs on the opposite lentil (**e–f**). Pick
up an 11º, a berry, and an 11º, and sew
through the next three Bs (**f–g**). Pick up
a B, an 11º, a berry, an 11º, and a B, and
sew through three Bs on the opposite
lentil (**g–h**). Pick up an 11º, a berry, and
an 11º, and sew through three Bs (**h–i**).
Continue sewing through a lentil, 15 Bs,
lentil, and ten 11ºs (**figure 5**).

4 Repeat steps 2–3 until you have
seven swags sewn in place. On the
seventh swag, end step 3 by sewing
through only seven 11ºs. Make sure your
thread is exiting the four 11ºs along the
bottom row. The tail ought to be sticking

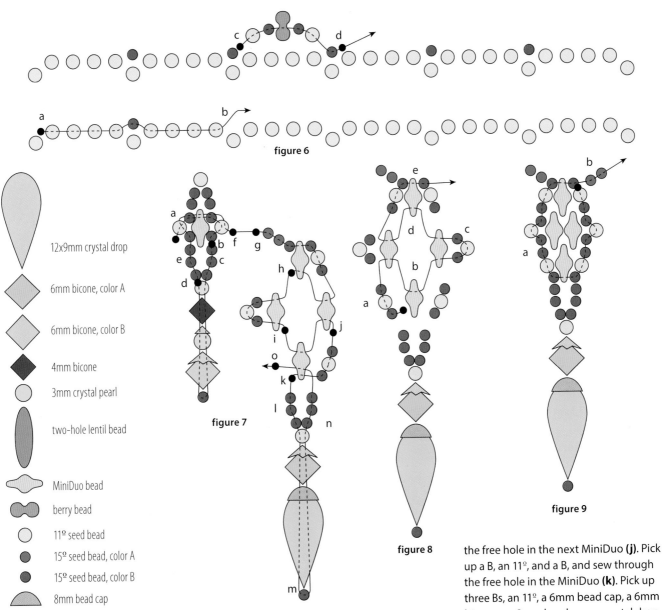

figure 6

12x9mm crystal drop

6mm bicone, color A

6mm bicone, color B

4mm bicone

3mm crystal pearl

two-hole lentil bead

MiniDuo bead

berry bead

11º seed bead

15º seed bead, color A

15º seed bead, color B

8mm bead cap

6mm bead cap

4mm bead cap

figure 7

figure 8

figure 9

out of the top row. Test the fit on the glass ball. If it is tight, sew a B between each group of four 11ºs along the bottom of the rectangles. If it is very loose, sew directly from one group of four 11ºs to the next group. End the thread along this bottom row of 11ºs (and maybe Bs).

5 Remove the stop bead, and thread a needle on the tail. Sew through four 11ºs. Pick up a B, and sew through the next four 11ºs **(figure 6, a)**. Repeat this stitch to sew seven Bs in place, and sew through the first B again. Pick up an 11º, a B, a berry, a B, and an 11º. Sew through the next B **(c-d)**. Sew seven of these little swags in place. Secure the thread in these swags.

6 Stretch and condition 2 yd. (1.8m) of thread. String a stop bead, and slide it to 12 in. (30cm) from the end.

7 Sew through an 11º, B, MiniDuo, B, 11º, and B **(figure 7, a–b)**. Pick up three Bs, an 11º, a 4mm bicone, a 4mm bead cap, a 3mm glass pearl, a 6mm bead cap, a 6mm bicone, and a B, and sew back through the bicone, bead cap, pearl, bead cap, bicone, and 11º **(c-d)**. Pick up three Bs, and sew through a B, 11º, B, MiniDuo, B, and 11º **(f)**.

8 Pick up two color A 15ºs, a B, a MiniDuo, a B, an 11º, a B, and a MiniDuo, and sew through the free hole in the first MiniDuo **(g-h)**. Pick up a MiniDuo, a B, an 11º, and a B, and sew through the free hole in the MiniDuo you just picked up **(i)**. Pick up a MiniDuo, and sew through

the free hole in the next MiniDuo **(j)**. Pick up a B, an 11º, and a B, and sew through the free hole in the MiniDuo **(k)**. Pick up three Bs, an 11º, a 6mm bead cap, a 6mm bicone, an 8mm bead cap, a crystal drop, and a B, and sew back through the drop, cap, bicone, cap, and 11º. Pick up three Bs, and sew through the bottom hole in the lowest MiniDuo **(l-m-n-o)**.

9 Pick up a B, an 11º, and a B, and sew through three MiniDuos **(figure 8, a–b)**. Pick up a B, an 11º, and a B, and sew through three MiniDuos **(c–d)**. Pick up an 11º, and sew through the top B, MiniDuo, and B **(e)**. Sew through the 11ºs and Bs that frame the MiniDuos, as well as the top and bottom MiniDuos **(figure 9, a)**. End by sewing through the top B, MiniDuo, and B. Pick up two As **(b)**.

10 Repeat step 7–9 to stitch seven MiniDuo panels with dangles. After you pick up the last two As, sew through an 11º, B, MiniDuo, B, and 11º. End the threads.

Supplies

SAPPHIRE BLUE COVER

- **1** 35mm glass ball ornament
- **6** 8mm fire-polished beads (sapphire)
- **6** 7x5mm fire-polished drops (milky sapphire)
- **72** two-hole crescent beads (CzechMates, transparent sapphire)
- **36** SuperDuo beads (pink suede)
- **30** berry beads (crystal luster)
- **12** 3mm crystal pearls (light gray)
- **2.5g** 11º seed beads (silver-lined crystal AB)
- **7g** 15º seed beads (blue iris)
- **12** 5mm bead caps (silver)
- **6** 3mm bead caps (silver)
- Size D thread of your choice
- Sizes 10 and 12 beading needles
- Stop beads
- Conditioner
- Thread snips

HARVEST COLORS COVER

- 8mm fire-polished beads: olivine
- 7x5mm fire-polished drops: olivine
- Two-hole crescent beads : honeydew
- SuperDuo beads: opaque beige luster
- berry beads: sparkling honey beige-lined
- 3mm crystal pearls: light gold
- 11º seed beads: green iris
- 15º seed beads: silver-lined root beer

SERAPHIM

What strikes you first about this ornament cover? Some people are drawn to the stylized feathers, while others notice the top first and are reminded of a little temple or shrine. Sometimes people are struck by the formal, almost rigid, look of it, which they sometimes describe as a sense of dignity.

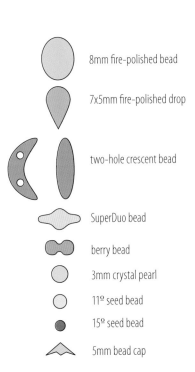

8mm fire-polished bead

7x5mm fire-polished drop

two-hole crescent bead

SuperDuo bead

berry bead

3mm crystal pearl

11º seed bead

15º seed bead

5mm bead cap

figure 1

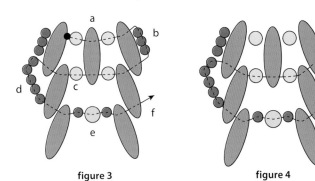

The points are on the back of the crescent

figure 2

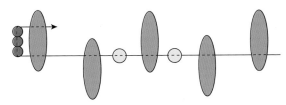

figure 3

figure 4

FEATHERS

1 Arrange 12 two-hole crescents as shown (**figure 1**). The instructions will say to pick each crescent by its top hole (TH) or its bottom hole (BH). Stretch and condition 1 yd. (.9m) of thread. Thread a needle. String a stop bead, and slide it to 8 in. (20cm) from the end. Pick up a crescent (BH), a crescent (TH), an 11º, a crescent (BH), an 11º, a crescent (TH), a crescent (BH), and three 15ºs, and sew through the top hole of the last crescent (**figure 2**).

2 Pick up an 11º, and sew through the free hole in the middle crescent. Pick up an 11º, and sew through the free hole in the last crescent. Pick up three 15ºs, and sew through two crescents, an 11º, crescent, 11º, and two crescents (**figure 3, a–b–c**). Pick up five 15ºs, and sew through the free hole in the nearest crescent. Pick up a crescent (TH), a 15º,

a 3mm pearl, a 15º, and a crescent (TH), and sew through the free hole in the nearest crescent (**d–e–f**). Pick up five 15ºs, and sew through two crescents, an 11º, crescent, 11º, two crescents, five 15ºs, two crescents, a 15º, pearl, 15º, and two crescents (**figure 4**).

3 Pick up five 15ºs, and sew through the free hole in the closest crescent (**figure 5, a–b**). Pick up a crescent (TH), an 11º, a crescent (TH), an 11º, and a crescent (TH), and sew through the free hole in the next crescent (**b–c**). Pick up five 15ºs. Sew through two crescents, a 15º, a pearl, a 15º, two crescents, five 15ºs, two crescents, an 11º, a crescent, an 11º, and two crescents (**c–d–e–f**).

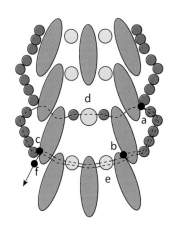

figure 5

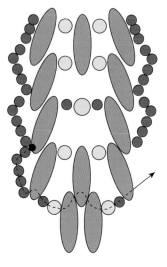

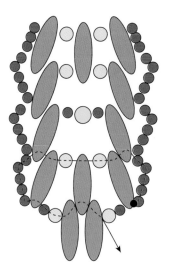

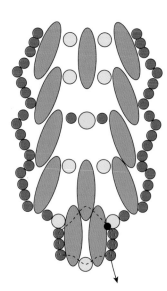

figure 6   figure 7   figure 8

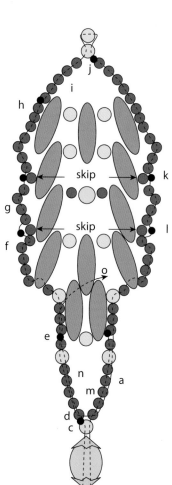

figure 9

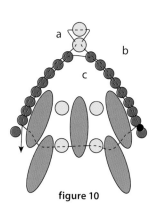

figure 10

4 Pick up five 15ºs, and sew through the free hole in the nearest crescent. Pick up a 15º, an 11º, and a crescent (TH). Sew through the free hole in the center crescent. Pick up a crescent (TH), an 11º, and a 15º, and sew through the free hole in the last crescent **(figure 6)**. Pick up five 15ºs, and sew through two crescents, an 11º, crescent, 11º, two crescents, five 15ºs, crescent, 15º, 11º, and three crescents **(figure 7)**.

5 Pick up three 15ºs. Sew through the free hole in the next crescent. Pick up an 11º, and sew through the free hole in the next crescent. Pick up three 15ºs, and sew through three crescents and three 15ºs **(figure 8)**. Pick up a 15º, 11º, five 15ºs, 11º, 5mm bead cap, 8mm fire-polished bead, 5mm bead cap, drop, 3mm bead cap, pearl, and 15º, and sew back through the pearl, cap, drop, cap, 8mm, cap, and 11º **(figure 9, a–b–c)**. Pick up five 15ºs, an 11º, and a 15º, and sew through three 15ºs, an 11º, 15º, crescent, and five 15ºs **(d–e–f)**. Skip a 15º and sew through four 15ºs **(g)**. Skip a 15º, and sew through seven 15ºs **(h)**. Pick up five 15ºs and two 11ºs, and sew back through the first 11º next to the 15ºs. Pick up five 15ºs, and sew through seven 15ºs **(i–j–k)**. Skip a 15º, and sew through four 15ºs **(l)**. Skip a 15º, and sew through five 15ºs, a crescent, 15º, 11º, four 15ºs, 11º,

and five 15ºs **(m)**. Skip the 11º, and sew through five 15ºs, an 11º, and four 15ºs. Secure the thread in the three crescents **(n–o)**. End the thread.

6 Remove the stop bead from the tail, and thread a needle. Sew through eight 15ºs and two 11ºs, and sew back through one 11º. Sew through the next five 15ºs in the hanger. Continue through three 15ºs, two crescents, an 11º, crescent, 11º, and two crescents. Sew through eight 15ºs. Skip the 11ºs, and sew through eight 15ºs **(figure 10, a–b–c)**. End the thread.

7 Repeat steps 1-6 to make five more feather components.

8 Stretch and condition 4½ ft. (1.38m) of thread. Thread on a needle ,and string a stop bead. Slide the stop bead to 12 in. (30cm) from the end. Pick up 36

figure 11

figure 12

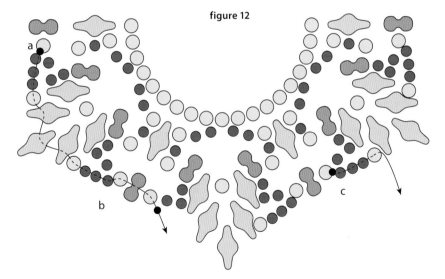

figure 13

11ºs, slide them down to the stop bead, and sew through them all again. Sew once more through the first bead. Pick up two 15ºs, an 11º, a SuperDuo bead, an 11º, and two 15ºs, skip five 11ºs, and sew through the sixth **(figure 11, a)**. Sew six of these swags in place. When done, sew through two 15ºs, an 11º, and a Super-Duo in the first swag. Pick up a 15º, and sew through the free hole in the Super-Duo. Pick up a 15º, and sew through the other hole of the SuperDuo, an 11º, two 15ºs, 11º, two 15ºs, 11º, and SuperDuo **(b–c)**. Repeat around. After adding two 15ºs to the last swag, sew through the beadwork to exit the bottom hole of a SuperDuo. Pick up an 11º, a berry bead, a SuperDuo, an 11º, a SuperDuo, a berry, and an 11º, and sew through the bottom hole in the next SuperDuo **(d–e)**. Repeat around. After you sew in the last swag, continue through an 11º, berry, Super-Duo, 11º, and SuperDuo.

9 Pick up two 15ºs. Sew through the free hole in the SuperDuo. Pick up two SuperDuos, and sew through the free hole in the next SuperDuo. Pick up two 15ºs, and sew through the other hole of the same SuperDuo, and the next 11º, SuperDuo, berry, 11º, Super-

Duo, 11º, berry, SuperDuo, 11º, and SuperDuo **(figure 12, a–b–c–d)**. Repeat these stitches five times. When done, continue through two 15ºs, four Super-Duos, and a 15º **(e)**.

10 Pick up a 15º, an 11º, a berry, an 11º, and a 15º, and sew through a 15º, four SuperDuos, and a 15º. Repeat this stitch five times. Continue through a 15º, 11º, berry, and 11º **(f–g–h)**.

11 Pick up three 15ºs and an 11º, and sew through the free hole in the next bottom SuperDuo. Pick up a Super-Duo, and sew through the free hole in the following SuperDuo. Pick up an 11º and three 15ºs, and sew through an 11º, berry, and 11º. Repeat these stitches five times. Continue through three 15ºs and an 11º **(figure 13, a–b–c)**.

12 Pick up four 15ºs, and sew through the free hole in the bottom Super-Duo. Pick up four 15ºs, and sew through an 11º and three 15ºs. Pick up three 15ºs, and sew through the top 11º in a feather. Pick up three 15ºs, and sew through three 15ºs and an 11º. Repeat these stitches five times **(figure 14, a-b-c)**. Continue through the first four 15ºs you sewed in place for this step **(d)**.

13 Pick up three 15ºs, and sew through the next four 15ºs. Pick up four 15ºs, and sew through a 15º, 11º, and 15º **(figure 15, a–b)**. Pick up four 15ºs, and sew through four 15ºs **(c)**. Repeat these stitches five times. End the thread.

14 Remove the stop bead, and thread a needle onto the tail. Sew through three 11ºs, pick up a 15º, an 11º, a berry, an 11º, and a 15º, skip five 11ºs, and sew through the next 11º. Repeat this stitch five times. Continue through a 15º, 11º, and berry **(figure 16, a–b–c)**.

15 Pick up a 15º, an 11º, a berry, an 11º, and a 15º, and sew through the next berry **(d)**. Repeat this stitch five times. End the thread.

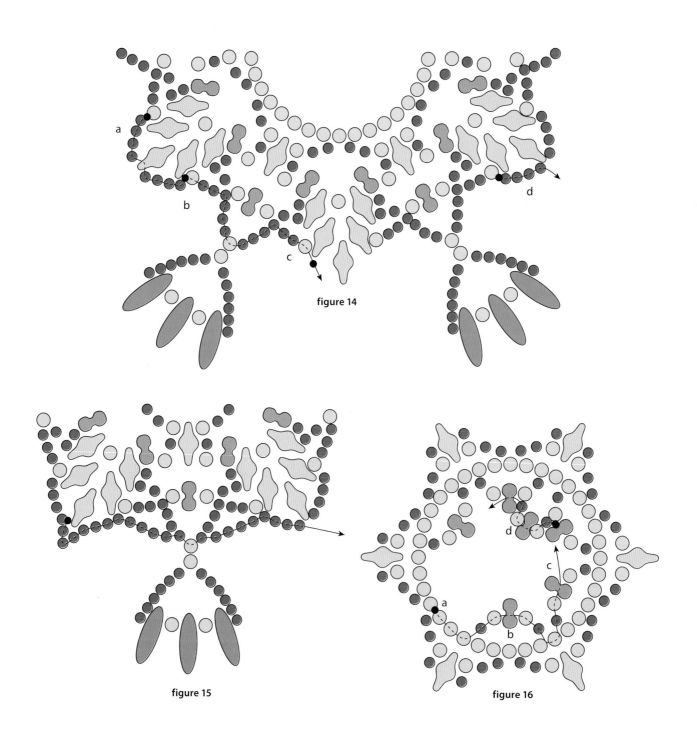

figure 14

figure 15

figure 16

make this lovely wreath
See page 36

ACKNOWLEDGMENTS

Many people helped me learn to write instructions over the years, and I am grateful to each of you for the time you spent in my classes. Grateful thanks to Melinda at Starman Beads for providing me with many, many beads and thank you to Barry at Caravan Beads for providing me with test samples. Special thanks belong to Erica Barse at Kalmbach Media for telling me about this ornament book which is, really, a dream come true. Thank you, Lisa Schroeder, for your inspired art direction and Bill Zuback, for your keen photographic eye, which brought this dream to life.

Heartfelt thanks to you, Nedda Rovelli, for your time and patience while shooting the process shots.

ABOUT THE AUTHOR

Thomasin "Alyx" Alyxander has been beading for a really long time. This is her second book with Kalmbach, and her instructions have been published in *Beadwork*, *Bead&Button*, and *Making Jewellery* magazines. For several years she has been one of Starman's Trendsetters. She has taught at the Bead&Button Show and been a finalist in BeadDreams. Because she is painfully shy, she is unlikely to tell you any of this if you ever meet her in person. You can find her on facebook at facebook.com/ubeadquitous or facebook.com/Component_Stitching.

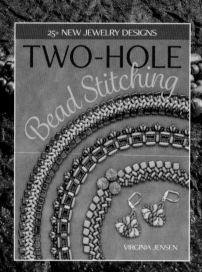